CARL RAKOSI: POEMS 1923–1941

Books by Carl Rakosi

Selected Poems (New Directions, 1941)
Amulet (New Directions, 1967)
Ere-Voice (New Directions, 1968)
Ex Cranium Night (Black Sparrow Press, 1975)
My Experiences in Parnassus (Black Sparrow Press, 1977)
Droles de Journal (The Toothpaste Press, 1981)
The Collected Prose of Carl Rakosi
(National Poetry Foundation, 1983)
The Collected Poems of Carl Rakosi
(National Poetry Foundation, 1986)
Poems 1923–1941 (Sun & Moon Press, 1995)

CARL RAKOSI

Poems 1923–1941

Edited by Andrew Crozier

SUN &
MOON

CLASSICS

64

SUN & MOON PRESS

LOS ANGELES • 1995

Sun & Moon Press
A Program of The Contemporary Arts Educational Project, Inc.
a nonprofit corporation
6026 Wilshire Boulevard, Los Angeles, California 90036

This edition first published in paperback in 1995 by Sun & Moon Press
10 9 8 7 6 5 4 3 2 1
FIRST EDITION
©1995, 1967 by Callman Rawley
Editorial matter and Introduction ©1995 by Andrew Crozier
Biographical material ©1995 by Sun & Moon Press

This book was made possible, in part, through an operational grant from the
Andrew W. Mellon Foundation, through a production grant from the
National Endowment for the Arts and through contributions to
The Contemporary Arts Educational Project, Inc.,
a nonprofit corporation

Cover: *Magnetische Landschaft* (*Magnetic Landscape*), Sigmar Polke
[Acrylic and ferrous mica on canvas], Raschdorf Collection
Cover Design: Katie Messborn
Typography: Guy Bennett

LIBRARY OF CONGRESS CATALOGING IN PUBLICATION DATA
Rakosi, Carl [1903]
[Callman Rawley]
Poems 1923–1941 / Carl Rakosi;
edited by Andrew Crozier.
p. cm — (Sun & Moon Classics: 64)
Includes bibliographical references and index.
ISBN: 1-55713-185-6, $12.95
I. Title. II. Series.
PS3535.A415A6 1995
811'.54—-dc20
94-46851 CIP

Printed in the United States of America on acid-free paper.

Contents

A Cautionary Note To The Reader From The Author 7

Editorial Introduction 11

Poems 1923–1941 33

Appendix: Unpublished, Never Completed,
    and Revised Poems 147

Notes 183

Index of Titles and First Lines 203

A CAUTIONARY NOTE TO THE READER
FROM THE AUTHOR

Readers of my very earliest poems need to be cautioned
that when these poems were written, in the early 1920s,
literary posturing was so prevalent, so much the natural
climate of writing, that it was not even noticed as pos-
turing. It took me a little time to realize that I too had
been posturing. For example, who was the young man
who wrote in "Gigantic Walker," "God, if I were up so
high…" etc. Was I ever that simple minded or pure
hearted? And did I really mean what I was saying?

Similarly in "The Holy Bonds," "My bride presents
me with a chart of gall…" etc. I wrote that when I was
just beginning to date girls. How could I have known
anything about marriage then? And what was the poem's
tragic note all about? I must have picked that note up
in my reading at the time and was so much a creature
of it that it never occurred to me that it might be insin-
cere. When it eventually did, of course I stopped.

This did not happen, however, until I had lived
through the phase of discovering literature, a phase all
writers have to go through, a phase that is as much a
voyage of discovery as any other. Which is to say that it

is legitimate. And that tragic note, so common among very young poets, was a malady I was suffering from too; and a case could be made, therefore, for claiming that the note was perfectly sincere.

I was dismayed, too, in reading proofs to find so many heavy Christological references and symbols. I was never religious, and I'm not a Christian. Again I can only account for it as the product of my reading. It is not until page 56 that, from where I stand now, I recognize myself and it's clear sailing.

All I'm saying is that if the reader so far is on my wave length, a little forbearance on his part will be necessary at the beginning in order to make Mr. Crozier's historical ordering of my early poems work. The chances are, however, that unless the reader's a literary critic, he will be on his own wave length, not mine, for he does not come to these early poems with my self-deprecating baggage. After all, my attitude toward these poems is not a part of them. In fact, they are no longer even a part of me. They stand there as givens. If they appeal to him, he has become convinced that the author was sincere and meant what he said, so what difference does it make to him whether they came early or late in the author's development?

Put another way, once a poem has been published, the exclusive relationship between an author and his poem has been severed and what remains, depending on the poem, is a relationship that ranges from secondary to practically zero. The poem then can be said to speak for itself and the matter is strictly between it and the reader. If it sounds sincere to him, therefore, it *is* sincere.

Finally, a word about the great trouble and labor Mr. Crozier has gone to in tracing and collecting my earliest work from many obscure little magazines of the time and the meticulous care with which he has restored my past, which I had lost and in a sense discarded... unfinished fragments, trial balloons, precepts on the fly...and the extraordinary acumen and insight with which he restored my long poem, "The Beasts." I am not sure I deserve such consideration since I have always maintained that the past is past, even to memory, and that for the writer only the present matters. Which is also true for the reader, of course, but his present, when he is reading a poem, is the author's past, and when those two come together, anything can happen.

With that, I leave the field gratefully to Mr. Crozier and the reader.

CARL RAKOSI

EDITORIAL INTRODUCTION

Found: A Modern Masterpiece

How much of modernism went unenacted in its permanent record of published works? Not all that much, perhaps, but one important omission to note in the list of America's classic modern texts is the collection of Carl Rakosi's poems which To, Publishers, and later the Objectivist Press, intended to publish.[1] How far Rakosi himself proceeded with this intention is open to doubt, but the prospect of collecting his work in the early 1930s was serious enough for him to have discussed with Margery Latimer, his literary confidante, the wisdom of publishing with a non-commercial imprint, and to inquire about other possible publishers.[2] We can assume that the unpublished book would have embodied and given shape to his first decade of writing and publication at a point when he was at the zenith of his early development as a poet. We can also be certain that, although he wrote only a few more poems during the remainder of the Thirties before falling silent (the alternative was literary obscurity) for decades, in the way of other "Objectivist" poets, the missing book would not, in significant respects, have resembled this one, although just what its difference might have been (or yet its consequences for Rakosi's subsequent career) is beyond conjecture. This edition of Rakosi's early poems cannot attempt to capture the moment of confident self-appraisal which marks a mature and deliberate first book, and is in any case sixty years too late for that. Instead it offers, without significant inflection or emphasis, the annals of Rakosi's career from 1923 to 1941.

Despite history, nevertheless, it does have something of the character of a chronologically belated first book, for what it emphatically is not is a retrospective issue of juvenilia. It is, to the contrary, a return to make good a major historical omission. Rakosi is well known now, among other things, as one of the "Objectivist" poets, the associate of George Oppen, Charles Reznikoff, and Louis Zukofsky. This group may be a construction of the late Sixties, a differentiation among the poets (including T.S. Eliot and Whittaker Chambers) who published as "Objectivists," but it nonetheless has historical presence, and yet of the four only Rakosi is not known by his work of the "Objectivist" epoch, which until now has been unavailable except in substantially revised forms. Thus the work on which Rakosi's historical status is predicated, as one of that distinctive group of second generation modernists, has remained virtually unknown, in an extraordinary intra-historical lacuna. Some of Rakosi's readers will have seen his *Selected Poems* (1941) and been misled by it, for it is a valedictory gesture in which his early poems received a high-contrast treatment as cameos and vignettes; others, perhaps, will have come across some of the poems in ones and twos in contemporary anthologies or the files of old magazines. Here for the first time, however, the poems Rakosi wrote as an "Objectivist," together with his other poems of the 1920s and 1930s, are brought together in one place in the original versions. To be able to read Rakosi thus historically is both to discover his true pedigree and to see his *Collected Poems* in the new light of its textual derivation. The reader is thus called to perform a double duty, both to attach Rakosi to the real historical past of modernism, and to reread the later Rakosi who has (no doubt partly in debt to the vicissitudes of history) been able to keep his text freely at his disposal as its own creative resource. Some readers may find that the poems collected here enable them to extend their historical understanding of Rakosi in a new and seamless unity. Others may find that the two phases of Rakosi's career remain distinct (such is my opinion) but that here at last the vigour and resourcefulness of its early phase are brought fully into view. But readers, being readers, will decide for themselves, and however that may be, here is a virtually unknown collection of original poems which, in excess of the sheer pleasure they afford, will extend significantly our knowledge of the repertoire of modernism and our historical understanding of the "Objectivists."

It would be inappropriate here to offer a critical appraisal of poems now for the first time seen all together, or to analyse their conditions of meaning, but it may be helpful to outline a more connected historical and bio-graphical narrative of their production than can be pro-vided by editorial annotation, even if only to restore to them something of their historical aura. Rakosi's career as a poet is interlocked with his life as an American: the two identities have a common dynamic and are shaped by the same historical forces. Thus if in the following account I discern distinct stages in Rakosi's early poetic career, these are also stages of assimilation and resis-tant self-assertion in the life of a foreign-born Ameri-can citizen, whose English is the language of the exter-nal, social horizon, rather than the home, yet also the language of the autonomous self—a linguistic paren-thesis around the family all the more noteworthy in a poet the epoch of whose first maturity was marked both by a strident ideological opposition of the individual and the collective, on the one hand, and on the other by a no less ideological inscription of the domestic unit as the embodiment of the American way.

Narratives of Jewish immigrant sons are typically records of cultural trauma, implicitly the simultaneous shocks of leaving the ghetto and discovering America. They are also strongly Oedipal, with a current of feel-ing flowing more generously to the mother, in her slower domestic adaptation, than to the father who is from the first exposed to America in the workshop and on the street. But it is clear from Rakosi's autobiographi-

cal memoir that the siblings of both parents had assimi-
lated to the dominant culture of Germany and Austria-
Hungary and, indeed, that uncles on both sides of the
family were Christian converts.[3] And although Rakosi's
father was a classic instance of the economic migrant,
he remarried while Rakosi was raised at home in Hun-
gary, until his seventh year, by maternal grandparents.
Thus Rakosi's American biography, dating from his ar-
rival at Ellis Island in 1910, concerns the school yard,
the street, and the public library far more than it does
the family home (also his father's place of business)
which asserts a double constraint of sentiment and ob-
ligation, in aspect perhaps already less Jewish than its
own version of immigrant frugality and self-reliance.
All of which is no more than to say that the drama of
Rakosi's biography is essentially personal (in a way
which an infantile memory of maternal abandonment
fully anticipates), and one on to which little is to be
projected except the narrative of poetic self-realisation.
English is already his language of self-affirmation, as
native as pugnacious self-defence, but also the instru-
ment of self-determination as one who lives by reading
and writing. In his early poetic self-isolation, therefore,
Rakosi's Jewishness is something identical rather than
an identity socially confirmed; not a trope for poetic
selfhood but, as it were, something recuperated and,
on occasion, expressed in it. Throughout his life poetry
appears to have been for Rakosi a desire and a commit-
ment potentially at odds with the needs of work and

economic security. Yet in both domains there is an avidity for different modes of experience (his acquisitive lexical habits are an index of this) which is nevertheless fastidious, and which may serve to explain the eventual determination of the career as a social worker and family therapist (even though at a crucial moment this was dictated by urgent necessity) in which his early poetic career was eventually extinguished. But for three years at the University of Wisconsin (1921–24) he was able to be unequivocally a poet, and there, the thematics of poetic isolation notwithstanding, he formed one of an out-of-the-ordinary and sparky literary circle with Kenneth Fearing, Leon Serabian Herald, and Margery Latimer. The most important feature of this group was that its local dissidence gave its members access to two quite distinct literary situations. Unexceptionally as student writers they published in student magazines, standing out against a pervasive tone of genteel mediocrity and prejudice. At the same time, as literary outsiders, their affinity was with the dispersed and international avant garde (as Rakosi's translations of Louis Aragon in his own magazine, *The Issue*, bear witness.)[4] In their generation, and situated as they were in the heartland of provincial conformity, the avant garde inclined inevitably to the left in politics, but a left which retained many traces of pre-war American socialism. Thus we find Rakosi publishing both in *The Little Review, Two Worlds, Exile,* and *transition,* and in *The Liberator, The Nation,* and *New Masses.* These two situations were successively complementary: inside and outside the university, the literary and the political avant garde, each the figure to another's ground. Rakosi's affiliation to the literary avant garde was able to sustain him as a poet (and perhaps at the same time contributed to divide him from the other members of his university circle) for several years after he left Wisconsin, until the next stage of his early career terminated when he moved to Texas in 1928, in what was on the face of it a willed act of poetic abnegation.

Rakosi's autobiographical memoir suggests that on graduation in 1924 and in need of a job he drifted into social work only to find a wide field of employment open to him, one which he enjoyed but found almost excessively stimulating, and which directed him toward new types of intellectual and professional formation. But for the time being social work offered freedom of movement, a migrant habit of work which took him to Cleveland, New York, Milwaukee, and Boston, as well as back to Madison. The family home in Kenosha served as a postal base, as it was to once again when he re-emerged as a poet after 1930. But in Texas from 1928, as he reported to Margery Latimer when their correspondence resumed with his resumption of publication, he turned in on himself while he cast about for a different professional orientation in university teaching, in law, in medicine. Social disgust, and social inhibition, put paid to the first and second options, but by 1932 he had completed preliminary courses for a degree in medicine. In the meantime he had not been forgotten as a poet, and late in 1930 Louis Zukofsky asked him to contribute to the "Objectivists" number of *Poetry* (February 1931). Zukofsky's act of recognition confirmed Rakosi's relation to the modernism of Pound, Williams, Stevens, and Moore, and moved him, for a few years, from the fringe of international modernism to the center stage of a project to site modernism in America itself. Emerging now into the full light of his poetic generation Rakosi was, in many respects, its star. With the exception of Crane, who by his linguistic habits was on the periphery of this new alignment of generations, as Zukofsky cogently recognised, Rakosi's publications were the most numerous and in the most prestigious places.[5] He perhaps had not been writing, but he had a backlog of unpublished work, was writing again, and the new work drew on the technical knowledge of his recent scientific studies as well as his varied life experience.

1931 and 1932 were the high point in Rakosi's early career. He was connected with the most resolutely intelligent tendency in American poetry, which enjoyed the reflected prestige and also the collaboration of a senior generation of modernist poets. He renewed old literary contacts and acquired new ones. *Poetry* was open to him, and he published in a new crop of substantial magazines: *Contact, Hound and Horn, Pagany,* and *Symposium*. But this flourishing situation was also modernism's Indian summer in America, and for Rakosi personally 1932, which was to have marked a fresh departure, turned out in actuality to be a year of traumatic change. It is worth trying to identify the different strands, historical, ideological, and personal, twisted together here. The Depression removed the economic foundations of his sector of the literary world: its magazines ceased to be financially viable. At the same time, for as long as they were able to continue, most of them turned toward the literary program of the left (*Pagany* is a striking example) and thus Rakosi and the other "Objectivists" found themselves increasingly isolated. Although their politics were of the left they held aloof from its artistic debates, and if their poems incorporated elements of the theoretical discourse of Marxism they did not do so under the guise of proletarian writing. Rakosi himself was anxious to see his work collected in book form because he was about to abandon four years of his life to a medical qualification, even while comparing his own prospects unfavorably to those which had faced Williams at the outset of his medical career. This, after all, was what the Texas years had all been for. But while history inexorably unfolded in the shape of economic calamity and political polarisation, Rakosi's intentions were thwarted. He was unable at the final hour, for financial reasons, to continue his medical training, and turned once again to social work, this time in Chicago.

Rakosi no longer had to suspend his life as a poet, but through the same combination of circumstances his poetic ambition was moderated. No book of his was published. His most ambitious poem, "The Beasts," which he had worked on for more than a year (the scale of its ambition can be gauged from the version in the Appendix) could only be published in an abbreviated form, although he was able to retrieve and put to other use passages removed from it. "The Beasts" was the site also of another conflict. Zukofsky had impugned its lack of determinate historical direction and, by implication, its quality of tenderness, which we can understand in terms both of its range of human reference and its perception of our species as one among others, including those primitive life forms studied by marine biologists. At the same time Zukofsky was drawing attention to the taut brevity of Williams's two and three line lyric stanzas, and it was toward this example that Rakosi's practice now turned. The formal logic is clear, although the stages of this process appear to have been simultaneous rather than successive.

The reception of Zukofsky's *An "Objectivists" Anthology* (1932) was symptomatic of the changing situation. Its expatriate origin cannot have helped, and to both left and right (the latter represented by the rational formalism promoted in *Hound and Horn* by Yvor Winters) it seemed an anachronism. The half-life of Objectivism was proving to be rather short. Rakosi continued to publish in 1933 and 1934, but in marginal places, the fag-end records of modernist enthusiasm. Then nothing, apart from the regional anthology *Poetry out of Wisconsin* (1937), until the *Selected Poems* of 1941. While in Chicago he drew close to the Communists.[6] In 1933 he returned to the South, this time to New Orleans, working for the Federal Transient Bureau and then at Tulane University. From 1935 to 1940 he was in New York, still in social work, and during the last two years of this period he took a Master's degree in social work at the University of Pennsylvania, where he came under the influence of the ideas of Otto Rank. But although he did not publish he continued to write, and attempted to reproduce inside his poetry a version of the Popular Front politics of the period. Some poems in *Selected Poems* are of this type, and transcriptions of unfinished poems of a more deeply felt political cast are included in the Appendix. He belonged to the League of American Writers, attended its meetings, and was one of the "Other Writers" who expressed their support for the Spanish Republic and condemnation of Fascism in the League's pamphlet *Writers Take Sides*.[7] For the first time since his student years at Madison Rakosi found himself in an actual literary milieu.

What appears to have moved him to collect his poems for publication was, once again, the prospect of further professional commitment. In 1940 he moved to St. Louis where, newly married, and about to start a family, he had taken a new post. He asked Kenneth Fearing's advice about the wisdom of paying to have a book published.[8] Then, late in 1940, he approached James Laughlin, whose recently established imprint New Directions was publishing Williams and Pound and thus continuing the work of To, Publishers and The Objectivist Press. Laughlin offered to publish him in the first series of "The Poet of the Month". For his *Selected Poems* Rakosi chose almost exclusively poems from the Thirties, which were subjected to an extreme version of the treatment previously accorded to "The Beasts": short excerpted passages were titled and presented in stark isolation, or passages from several poems were juxtaposed in an emphatic manner. It was as if Rakosi denied poetic imagination and discourse and reduced his writing to its elemental moments of linguistic vitality and discrete perception.

And that, it might appear, was to be that, until the publication of *Amulet* a quarter of a century later. But there is a coda to this narrative showing that Rakosi remained on the tenterhooks of poetic desire and economic necessity. In 1942 he made an unsuccessful application to the Guggenheim Foundation for a Fellowship to enable him to write poetry, "free from the crippling effects of social work." "I would write about the contemporary scene, for that is where my interest lies, and I would handle it with as scrupulous a realism as the imagination could bear." If he "ran out of poetry" he had notes he wanted to work up on personal "psychoanalytic data regarding the origin of writing."[9]

Rakosi's interest in the evidence his psychoanalysis bore for his writing is revealing at this point. He returns to his origin as a writer precisely when, as husband and father, he has returned to the family scene around which his self-affirmation in language had previously looped. It would appear that the tension between realism and the imagination not only reproduces that between work and writing but has deeper resonances. That such tensions were objective, and exacted a price in the short term, there can be no doubt, but we should not think of them biographically in terms of a thwarted or damaged career. We can turn to the *Collected Poems*, as well as to the poems gathered here, for evidence of the creative productivity of these very tensions.

If we look no further than the conflict between poetry and work, thrown sharply into relief by Rakosi's history of publication between 1923 and 1941 as it may appear to be, his career might seem damaged and his art vulnerable. But to do so is to give implicit assent to a modernist myth of the poet of the sort promulgated, for example, in Pound's repeated interventions on behalf of writers he thought needed rescuing from financial exigency. This is to insert the relations of aristocratic patronage within the quite different social ethos of the artist as professional in a way which ignores the real social relations of the poet in the age of popular media (which began longer ago than we often think) and thus ignores the actual creative matrix of modern poetry. Equally it ignores the fact that a writing block or inhibition is part of the phenomenology of writing. The point in relation to Rakosi is that his stallings, hesitations, and diversions, even his bitter complaints about his situation as a writer, belonged fully to his writing, and contributed to it beyond any call for alleviation. It is idle to bewail the notion that a poet has not produced more when he has already written much. If one were tempted to deprecate any aspect of his career it should be borne in mind that Rakosi never committed the authentic sin against poetry of the contemporary poet, foreswearing it in the name of a more adult or a more fully social self.

So we should not approach the poems gathered here at last as a faded historical document, lightly tinged with pathos, but as a substantial body of fully achieved writing which has its own clear figuration. The Rakosi encountered here can hold his own with other poets whose body of work is small but select, for despite some little evidence of textual afterthought and vacillation the poems are above all notable, despite their linguistic flamboyance and enflamed sexiness, for their considered finality. Both in their local texture and as complete utterances they are decisively what they are, and entirely deliberate in what they effect. There is little journeyman work or routine engine maintenance, no poem that the reader will be tempted to skip. Each makes its own contribution to the complete achievement. And this achievement, across its historical turns and occlusions, has a characteristic consistency. We can trace an imaginative act of inscription and exposure throughout, from "Jacob Gold" ("What phantom men would wink behind his face") to "The Beasts" ("wheels and anchors in its skin") to, finally, "Dedication" ("the chubb, his guts out…and fresh herbs in his belly"). This act is repeated formally in the satirical poems of the 1920s, and in the lists and juxtapositions of the 1930s: an act which, despite its frequent passages of specular scrutiny, is not that of the dispassionate gaze, but an uncovering and construction of meaning, the conception and interpretation of experience at once intimately given and utterly strange.

This edition and its sources

This edition is that awkward thing, an *editio princeps* without the authority of a manuscript original. The editorial function has been both to shape the corpus and establish the text without a tradition to follow. It is also an edition for which the authority of the writer's "final intention" cannot be invoked, even were that specious unity taken as the last word in editorial decorum. Many of Rakosi's early poems have been carried through successive stages of revision to take their place in the singular unity of his *Collected Poems*, where the versions (not always apparent as such) which stand for them in that deeply meditated version of a lifetime's accomplishment register barely the trace of their origins. The purpose of this edition is to provide as far as possible a reliable account of what Rakosi wrote in the 1920s and 1930s. I have, needless to say, consulted him throughout my work.

Hardly any of Rakosi's manuscripts have survived from this phase of his career. The only ones he kept himself were drafts for unfinished poems from the late 1930s, now in his archive at the University of Wisconsin. With few exceptions the manuscript copies of his published poems appear to have disappeared into the oblivion of the printing house. So this is, for better or worse, an edition based primarily on printed sources. These sources, the little magazines of the period for the most part, have by their very nature an inconsistent and heterogeneous character, and do not always provide the most reliable of guides to the writer's intentions at the time. The one exception might have been Rakosi's *Selected Poems*, but this brings with it problems of a rather different sort. Rakosi's reworking of most of the contents produced effects which he quickly regretted and which this edition, by its very purpose, will correct. For these reasons I have treated *Selected Poems* as a source only for poems published there for the first time. But I have also included separately in an Appendix, with a number of other pieces which seem best to belong in such a place, its cut and spliced versions of earlier poems.

The sources that I have had to use present a number of problems arising from the conventions of publishing at a time when the attitudes of writers to their manuscripts, and of editors and printers to copy, were somewhat different to what they are today. It was either a laborious or a costly business to produce multiple clean copies before the epoch of the photocopier, and writers could often rely on proofs for the final correction of their work. That was in the days of moveable type, today's unimaginable luxury. But before the writer had sight of proof an editor's or a printer's notions of correctness might intervene, indeed such correction of the writer's copy might be taken for granted and even relied on. In Rakosi's case certain features of his writing caused his manuscripts to fall foul of the demands of house styles: hyphens were inserted to dislocate his compound words; his lines of dots were given the connective authority of colons. The few manuscripts that I have been able to locate show careful as well as considered preparation (although there are cases of full points and parentheses being superimposed); some also bear the marks of intrusive editorial alteration of significant detail. Even without supporting manuscript evidence the conclusion seems inescapable that some of the printed sources on which this edition depends were corrected in similar ways. Where a manuscript differs from its printed version I have been guided by it, but where it stands at some remove from the copy text I have recorded differences in the notes. Differences between this edition and its copy texts are noted, as are significant textual variants in other sources, but I have not in general attempted to describe differences of textual disposition on the page. Nor have I attempted to make alterations in accordance with a theory of Rakosi's proper style and conventions, although there has been occasion to prefer one printed source to another on such grounds.

The notes list all manuscript and printed sources that

I have been able to locate. Rakosi's correspondence mentions several poems which I have not been able to trace: "the rhubarb leaves one," "The Meeting," "Black Sun," "We," "The Black Matter," "The Hosts," "Faces on Fifth Avenue," "The Daily Press," "Composition," "Both Ways," "Address to Oneself." In view of his habits of composition it is more than likely that some of these have found their way into this edition under other titles, but it is also possible that there remain other poems from the period 1923–41 to be found.

I have included in the notes what information I have been able to discover about a poem's date of composition. The relative character of this information, such as it is, will make clear my reasons for not attempting to arrange the poems according to a chronology of composition. They are, instead, arranged according to chronological order of publication, and this, I believe, supplemented by the information provided in the notes, affords a rough and ready guide to the order of their composition. *Selected Poems* is the subject of a separate note.

Acknowledgments

First and foremost acknowledgment is due to the Poetry Collection of the Lockwood Memorial Library, State University of New York at Buffalo, where I began to collect Carl Rakosi's poems in 1964. More recently, since Carl Rakosi authorised me to prepare this edition, Robert Bertholf, Curator of what is now the Poetry/Rare Books Collection, kindly provided photocopies by which to check some of my early transcriptions. The late George Butterick, my friend and fellow student at Buffalo, gave invaluable advice when Curator of Literary Archives at the University of Connecticut. I wish also to record my particular indebtedness to Yvonne Schofer of the Memorial Library, University of Wisconsin-Madison, for unstinted assistance over several years.

Other friends and colleagues have assisted me in different ways at various times, and I wish to thank Barry Ahearn, Joan Benning, Michael Heller, Eric Homberger, D.S. Marriott, Douglas Oliver, Jeffrey Peterson, Stephen Rodefer, Anthony Rudolf, Robert M. Ryley, Charles Swann, and Keith Waldrop. I am grateful to James Laughlin for providing me with copies of letters to him from Carl Rakosi, and allowing me to quote from them.

Acknowledgment for permission to publish or quote from materials in their collections is gratefully made to the University of Chicago Library, the University of Delaware Library, the John Simon Guggenheim Memorial Foundation, the Library of the University of North Carolina at Chapel Hill, the Memorial Library, University of Wisconsin-Madison, and the Beinecke Rare Book and Manuscript Library, Yale University. Acknowledgment for assistance of various sorts is also due to the Office of the University Registrar, University of Chicago, the Houghton Library, Harvard University, the Manuscripts Department, Lilly Library, Indiana University, the London School of Economics Library, Seattle Public Library, the University of Sussex Library, the Harry Ransom Humanities Research Center, University of Texas at Austin, the Office of the Registrar, University of Wisconsin-Madison, and the Frumkin Memorial Collection, University of Wisconsin-Milwaukee Library.

I am grateful to the School of English and American Studies, University of Sussex, for grants from its research fund. My thanks to Margaret Reynolds for putting the manuscript on to computer disc come last, but my debt to her is by no means the least of those acknowledged here.

POEMS 1923–1941

Jacob Gold

What phantom men would wink behind his face?
They always wandered through their dusk-shawled place.
They had inscribed under his harried features
The lineaments of plants and forest creatures
To wound his flesh-hued image with a knife,
And prick the decent armor of his life.

He wondered if there was a Jacob Gold,
Or something else more primitively old.
He used to gaze into a glass and say,
"I think I met some Jacob Golds today."
Or, "Maybe nothing that I see is real:
Only the silken voice white nights reveal."

Old Jacob Gold had laughed at luxury,
And lived his body's Winter quietly.
He worked and bore the burdens of his race
As plainly as the wrinkles on his face.
Within his globe of years he only saw
A frieze of angels lighting stones of law.

The Old Men

I saw the knotted old men gaze
Into the snowing waters;
I saw them dream like bamboo stalks
Hung on the falling waters,
Falling like beauty forever.

No sun or moon will ever
Look in their hearts again;
No eyes or hearts of men.
But bees will suck an hour
In the cup of a new gold flower.

Gigantic Walker

God, if I were up so high,
Where you wade across the sky,
I'd scoop into your pool of blue,
And let the clear light trickle through.

Stoop, and lift me to your knees,
Gigantic Walker of the Skies;
Lend me your sun and all your eyes,
And I will make a poem of these.

Two Digging

Janik, a middle-aged Slovak, with a face as dull as thick paper, and a body too long for his legs, was coming home from work. A neighbor poked her head out of a window. She had waited a half hour for him and now her face was red with excitement, like a swollen biscuit. "Just imagine, your wife she took a job in the spring-room."

"Well, you old hen, still looking for trouble? You make far less noise in your husband's bed."

When he passed into the house, he decided that his wife had insulted him. As he could lose his temper at will, he threw his black cap at her, and felt outraged. He ran into Modovy's saloon. The bartender, with a paunch like a kettle, was wiping the counter. Janik shouted and waved his oily hands.

"If she fools with me, I'll break her bones. Do I deserve this after earning her bread and butter? She makes me crazy."

His face was whiter than ever. The bartender looked at him and filled two tumblers with schnapps. As Janik walked out, he whispered to himself:

"I'll fix her, the American lady!"

He whistled and felt good because the moon dipped

like a pretzel in blue wine. Far away a dark mass moved like a cloud. It sagged down on him with set features; it was an idea.

His wife shook him the next morning.

"Get up, Janik, get up."

She dressed and made sandwiches for the two of them. But he did not stir. He remembered their first days together in another factory town. She was waitress in a Greek restaurant where men expected something of the help. Her figure moved with long, sensual curves, while her features protested a cute innocence. Janik did not care about her liaisons, as long as he could have her. After ten years of married life, she still went out motoring with young men. Janik accepted his wife with the silence of a peasant; work was the heavy reality to him.

He saw her waddle down the steps with her dinner pail.

"Let her work if she wants to."

She could not understand the serious solidity of his character. How futile, he thought, for a woman to exhaust her prime in passion. All his life he had waited to concentrate the love of his body and mind on some beautiful abstraction. The shop machines beat him with fatigue. In the night a dream grew like an expectation. He had been a king and stood at the frontier of the world. His people waited on the mortal bank as he penetrated darkness. Long ebony pipes blew. He could not remember the adventures he had encountered, but his breath caught in their thrill.

When the whistles sounded, he dressed and sat an hour in his back yard. The ground was a firm gray, with a wood pile and iron tubing at the edges. After he had counted a dozen weeds he brought out his coal shovel from the basement and began digging. He sniffed at the raw onion smell.

"What you digging for, mister?"

A circle of boys were watching. He lifted the shovel menacingly.

"Get out of here; don't bother me."

After two hours his legs sank into a marshy bottom. He covered the hole and walked into the house, disappointed. He tore open the side of his mattress, where he had once sewn a hundred dollars, and deposited the money in a bank. It was past noon when he returned. Again he took his shovel and a lantern and walked with them beyond the city limits.

He went along the bank of a muddy creek, crossed an enclined bridge, reached the former resort of Casselburg. The building was owned by Peter Jacobs, a lonely old man of eccentric habits. In the summer he and his daughter, a school teacher, moved into the empty rooms. The silver birch canoe, reversed at the side of the house, took on a nickel plating in the strong sun. As Janik came up the path, the old man yelled a hello, and grumbled to his daughter. "Another one of them wops, uncivil as usual."

Janik selected a spot about a hundred yards from Casselburg, and digged until dark. Then he lit his lantern and set to work again. The woman watched the yellow suffusion from the doorway. She was tall and stiff, rather aristocratic with her delicate dark features. She turned to her father.

"Guess I'll go for a walk."

Here, in the evening, her devotion to the ideas of great men did not matter. She felt the slow charm of the moment, as she had often felt when sitting after school, thinking of nothing. She strolled over to the lantern and watched Janik's stern face and the tight muscles on his hands. Then she lay supine before him.

"What are you doing?"

He glanced at her with a sly look, as if he laughed over her wantonness, and mumbled something about his shovel. After she had walked away he turned all his attention to it.

In the house the old man sat down to the piano, before a folio of Chopin. His nocturne vibrated among the violet pines. The woman stopped where the lantern barely reached her. Slowly, with an inevitable motion, she removed her shoes and clothing. Janik bent his back to slice the earth with the shovel. Could he but reach the dark center of that expectation, and find a thing to satisfy his dream? Above his humid trench the cactus and the weeds, while the tall trunks shot out into a tapestry of cones and angles. Once his lantern bucked, as he had seen the Noctiluca in the late sea, and he caught sight of the woman, pale and motionless in an envelope of vapor. The blood warmed his nape. He stumbled forward and caught her in his tough arms. At last she was falling—falling!

Six Essays in Sentiment

1

Spin a dream of the woman you love.
She will glow and fade from the land
Like the fall of a shadow over the hand.
(The white leaf curls to dust above.)
On her account I slept in flame,
In a chapel, till my woman came.
She wept in her hands and went away.
(She had looked at my thousand dreams one day.)

2

We travelled through their walls,
The waters and I;
O sea of snowing heart,
We blew their graphite sky.
Our ship the Windy Years
(No steel or steam)
Broke off its silver cable
Of earthly dream.
Halloo it from the edge of dim horizons;
This mass of water turns on icy gears.

3

A thrush got snared on a humped pine tree;
All day he whistled of wind and sea.
In the plexus of white stars over my brow,
The shrill reed died on the swinging bough.
I made my bed in the house of night,
And thought no bird could sing without light.
But a star shakes gut, and the moon, a gong,
Though the throat of the bird is hushed in song.

4

You are far more beautiful
Than a crescent branch of light;
I will capture one as scull
For you to sail the seas of my sight.
You will woo the mango moon,
And pluck the star leaves from her hands;
You will chill the hot sun soon
And wring her heart out with your hands.
I saw God's agate fingers place
Your light in chapelries of space.

5

After Francis Jammes

O guardian angel abandoned
For this lovely body, white as a carpet of lilies,
I am alone today; take my hand.
O guardian angel abandoned
When my heart burst in the Summer of joy,
I am sad today; take my hand.
O guardian angel abandoned
When I trod the gold of forests with my careless feet,
I am poor today; take my hand.
O guardian angel abandoned
When I dreamed before the snow on the roofs,
I cannot dream now; take my hand.

6

The Son to His Choleric Father

This blood his ego gave —
My pity heal the blow;
Within my heart I vow
To hate him to his grave.
Proud father to a stone,
He will not ever know
The silence on his brow
Has eaten to my bone.

Plein-Air

The bridge-hands at the edge of the water,
Hoisting logs, planks, down the creek of slate,
Calling to the papaw sun,
Played a Sicilian monody
For two baby squirrels
Under a vertical willow shoot
To a neurasthenic jay
In feather of blue spleen.
The bird in bluing,
Clapped on a ground-twig,
Twitching his pate.
Like a purr of arrows
He shot to the red-oak.

My company in the woods included
            A bee,
        A zigzag fence,
        And Arno Holz.

Idyll of Seeds

("They Have Their Exits and Their Entrances")

Lost in the still hair of the pine,
My girl on a mat of leaf and stream,
With bamboo pipes to shake our tent,
And negro birds in the wood of dream.

I think the Syrinx fugue on a bough
Will fall wildly asleep some day,
And cisterns and cicadas chirr
To city women, dry-dugged now.

Imagine blood veined in their seeds,
And limbs locked in a mist of light;
And weeping on the coast of silence;
The child lifted from natal night.

(The master of the silver globes
Drew his great hair over my head.)
I slept in the lakelight of His globes;
I lay one instant with the dead.

Solstice and equinox of heat
And ice, aeons of fiery life
Sag like a vapor, and I sit—
In my sad cast, designed like lead.

Earth mixes in the Goya gloom,
Folding a fog quilt on the lover.
The player's seeds return to her
After a slow cycle of doom.

The Flowers of Gloom

Gray light bereaved the calm all day;
Now women flute into the night.
Oh what are the winds and what are the waves
To the silver wake of their sexless flight?

They fold their faces in violent whorl;
Their arms shall branch in willow bloom.
No seed in the pots of day
Can vie with the flowers of gloom.

They whistle of winds and water,
And plunge of final night:
"Beyond the sandaracs of pleached moon woods,
The winds and waters flux to the end of sight."

For Lothario

Lothario, I've ordered a winding sheet
Of butterflies for my arcane repose.

Think how my fiery limbs, sprung into pines,
Shall grieve this void storm of our land of fleas

Lothario, this is no comic role
To blunder through a vegetative fog,

And slave in deep crafts for some tedious weed.
Think of the leprous anguish in the hand

That wrote the metaphysics of the thrush,
And taints men with the holy vagueness of
The moon's phrase. Yes, the pantomime is off.
The chime of pallors from narcotic alps
Descends like satire on my dusty ears.

For the Processionals of Lust

This blond youth like an acolyte makes hue
of sober days, burns like an actor star.
The mountain sinks of void make sound he knew
while dreaming what the chords of cosmos are.
Some nights her lust lit music in his head.
(His love elicits sleep of primal sleep.)
Dreams were the evocations of her tread
across the pomp of evening platforms; these
were shows for dreams. The dusk returns her Greek
prose figure, while the oxwagons of thought
trek out to space. He cannot move or speak
and takes her shadow hair for lanterns wrought
of basalt glow. Wild fowl and apes and cavemen
wait with him through the starstream for a woman.

Creation

Do not come among these trees of lead.
When the apple blooms along the sky
of many berries, you will see the dead:
shadows and sour sprites in wood, the lean
of sagging flesh wade in the wet loam.

Dark angels shut their box upon these trunks;
the oakroots claw the underground for hue.
You will not pass the wild rim of your home,
nor ever feel the earth reach out a strong shoot.

Do not come into the forest of the world!

But if your legs dig through the ground like stone,
your straw hair grow on clouds, you will not fear
to shape the facile forms of blood and bone.
Because a woman plays a sleep guitar
on sober braids, it does not mean that she
has shaken every tone. You cannot hear
Bach in her hair, nor trap the Whistler lights.
You must compose all shifting forms to beauty.

Sittingroom by Patinka

I found Miss Levi in a plush repose,
counting the curves pitched in her portly mirrors
by seven bored and pygmy globes. Her floors
were tourmaline supporting topaz standards.
Moist for the mouthing of mild platitudes,
here evenings passed Venetian glasses and
oak planes through green transitions. Walnut backs
diffused her satin cases. She seemed faint,
ecstatic in her parlor sunsets, stamping
her wronged head on an old medallion.

The cisterns warbled the October rain
on afternoons. We listened into green
designs of gloom like sleepers. "Carl, I feel
the musings of profuse dim meistersingers."
Her meanings muffle dark interiors
which were an invocation to the sun.
"We mix with carbonates and corals on
pelagic passes where prawns sail like passions.
Sea-spiders hobble from my hair, my eyes
shall twinkle into octagons of frost."

She heard a subway of demotic voices,
scoffing at all unmusical dispassions.
Their basses settled in a dantesque laughter,
while icy faint buffoons profaned rich prescience.
She said a lodge of hairless ponderors
would stand in choir while the infant dawns
poured tea, to chant the aufklarung of men.
Obsessions died among her sweet liqueurs
and pungent bottles. She would stir cool coffee
and feel the messengers of void encroach.

While swallows chittered in the hush and light
and gray gulls skated ciphers over June,
a band of trumpets called a fierce refrain
for thud of blond divines from Palestine,
whose footsteps drowned the ariette of birds.
And when her schoolmen passed like prophecy
and mighty infants, she could not affront
their high detachment with her bungled pathos.
Their white feet were an exhalation of
the lovely sin of death for they were bawds.

The January of a Gnat

Snow panels, ice pipes, house the afternoon
whose poised arms lift prayer with the elm's antennae.
She has her wind of swift burrs, whose spiel is gruff,
scanning the white mind of the winter moon
with her blank miles. Her voice is lower than the
clovers or the bassviol of seastuff.

So void moons make a chaste anabasis
across the stalks of star and edelweiss,
while Volga nixies and a Munich six
o'clock hear in the diaphane the rise
of one bassoon. So the immense frosts fix
their vacant death, bugs spray the roots like lice.
High blizzards broom the cold for answer to
their ssh of vapors and their vowel ooo

Flora and the Ogre

Let her quince knees sag
and the toy arcs of the dew
and daisy
guide her mild feet,
her torso is no more to me than
the woodcut of a nun.

In a peignoir that snows to her ankles,
she paces the movement
of sun and dark,
and her step is like the pulse of lilies.

All motion blurs the scented yaw of her skirts...
(Linen like the subsiding of labials,
like the undertow in the veins.)
While the three tenses
faltered between her painful thighs,
a wind of scarves rose.
Will no briny thunderbrunt
or green chill
deliver me from naughty wishes?

The Holy Bonds

My bride presents me with a chart of gall
involving the designs we two create,
and seems to doubt me and to meditate
inviolacies her tears fail to recall.

She plans to promenade in grim attire
while I exploit the offices of hate,
and I shall keep still and regard the fire
and her chart, and add fuel in the grate.

My bride has issued from her private door
and bursts into a cold inverted laugh,
for she has found me humbled on the floor,
a sprig of ashes held between my teeth.
This she interprets as despair and chaff
conceding to her shabby bridal wreath.

Autumn in Dane County

I walked out ten miles on our mall of willows
to where the wild ducks skittered in the foam
of sunlight and the loud gusts on the lake
were scouring tides for a November home.

This water is the shanty where the winds
loaf, and a pale morgue for the stiff duck's float—
all fail, their hearts drained by the hunter's fire.
The dead birds flow now like a multiple boat.

Hokku

Old men and expunged
old men. Look! The bamboo stalks
hang on the rapids.

The Weaver spins gold.
The women of lust wash me,
broidered with sun-nerves.

The dates of light fall.
A bush breaks through the white walk.
O my shadow, sing!

Woods shake in the dark.
The winds blend. When shall I wake
to stir my fibers?

Shadows for Florida

Summer, the Negro's cabin was full of voices,
and the sawgrass pointed straight north toward the cities;
and I said: "Are you giving us a tune, brother?"

So he chanted: "Hosanna's in the cotton,
                and singing's in the citrus;
                there is singing with the blackbirds too;
                there is singing from the rocks.
                Should I sing from the rocks?
                Should I sing from the rocks
                if I can not find Jesus?"

Go on singing, brother, go on.
And the blackbird filled the palms.

While in the slack season the building tradesmen
quartered on the Eastern seaboard.
"Stick together, white men," I advised,
"Where else will you find so many voices?"
But they protested in a deep key:

58

"We don't hear anything;
nothing here but heat waves;
nothing here but scrub and dark children.
What are the voices about?
Are they with us?
Will they tell us about the snow on Main Street?"

Scriptural Program

1

The king of the Jews shall understand
that Yahweh is
   Lord of four kingdoms.
And these be their names:
there is the kingdom of fire
that is the compend of his word;
and the kingdom of the earth
of which men say that it was
Eden of the ancient books
(but now this no more
but those merchants of Palestine);
and the kingdom of the air
where the birds made offering to our Lord
for his benevolent attitude;
and finally there is the kingdom of water
that is the history of many seabirds
and winds
and sailors in
   their salty coffins.

And because of the awful torah and the ark,
our Lord is like the apex in the south,
and like the scepter of the north.

2

Is it only a stray dusk,
O dark youth,
heavy with psalms,
in the shelter of your devout hands?

Or an old discarded yearning
for exotic voids?

Or that gradual passage
of her hair
wherein the last Hebraic light
supremely retires.

3

Thine hair is the plucking of the strings
of the zithers of darkness.
Thine eyes build new sacristies
for the pyx of silence.
Thy mouth is a pouch
for the accents of queens.

In the foggy wilderness
is not thine heart
as important as the hermit-thrush?

My dear, thy words persist
like some remote ancestral oboe,
while the alien void recalls
the salty heat of barbarism.
And I flag in the brace of irony,
for the strokes of thine hand
  have nailed me to anguish.

4

Beloved,
now that your body is at my will,
and my wits stray,
and my arms hang oppressed,
I think of stripping the orchard.

At last, beloved,
your blissful thighs seemed
perished
in a long sting;
but the closed eyes,
the furious veins still
throbbed;
and I said,

"I have my lips below her wassailous armpits,"
and suddenly gloated at the thought
of breaking you to death,
you and your moist loins.

Beloved,
now your body is in my hands!

5

Lovely as the tomb is
and the pomp of flutes,
I do not brood on their account
but because I can not forget
the ceremony of the tetrarch's swans.
The time comes when the swans
attend his court,
traditional and sexless,
inviting the swansheer transit
of the beautiful one.
My beloved is timeless as the mirrors,
isolate as the frost
on the queen of swans.
Now that I have seen
the royal stones and fountains,
and the tetrarch's arrowbright attendants,
I say that my beloved is but a
mindful of whitebirds.

6

Sandalwood comes to my mind
when I think of thee
and the triumph of thy shoulders.
Greek chorus girls came to me
in the course of the day,
and from a distance,
in a smoke of clamour,
the Celtic vestals too.
But my Jewess brings me the Holy Land
and the sound of deep themes
in the inner chamber.
And there are pauses
where she is gravid with
dark ways and illness,
and the ovation of old books.
Therefore the prophets are angry
with her laden limbs,
and because of the coral of her two breasts.
But I have my lips upon them
and the song shall go on.

What metaphors for you,
Jewess of the palmcountry,
but what is already written of
wells and vineyards
and the fawneyes of the woodland.
Names come and go
but not the folly of an old Jew.

7

At Stagyra lies Saint Belle,
our Lady's niece,
and there lies also the body of Aristotle.
And you shall understand
that her bones are annointed with
the gum of plumtrees,
and that all men are used to attend
her grave on Lent.
And men say that in her youth
she was led into a garden of Caiphas
and there she was crowned with
the sweet thorn called barbariens.
But now this is no more
but a tablet seven cubits long
above her head,
on which the title is written
in Hebrew
Greek and Latin,
and the date when it was
laid in the earth.
And the body of Aristotle
stinketh too in a casket at Stagyra,
but the eyes are at Paris
in the King's chapel.
And nevertheless the emperor of Almayne
saith that he hath the eyes.
And I have oftentime seen them,
but they are greater than those at Paris.

Vitagraph

Out in God's country where men are men,
the terror of Red Gap used to ride on his
bulletsudden roan.
He was called God damn Higgins
and was said to have faith only in his gun,
his horse, and Denver Nan.
It turned out she was in cahoots with Gentleman Joe
who could shuffle a deck faster than you can count,
and one day the two of them cleaned the poor sucker
        out of his last red cent.
But it was the last time Gentleman Joe
hung his thumb into the armpit of his vest
and snickered behind his nibbled tooth pick,
for a masked stranger showed up in the barroom
that night, with his hand on his hip pocket.
Years later the reverend Marcus Whitney
pitched his tent in town,
And Denver Nan had her only chance to go straight,
And made good,
And married good deed Higgins,
And three cheers for the star spangled banner.
And how about God damn Higgins?
Oh he used to be hard all right.
He could draw a gun faster than any man in Arizona.

Characters

One of our brassy beefeaters
in grandstand on the continent
bares biceps to the gaping millions,
sinks shaft in market, pockets wheat
holds cornucopia of cash.
Cheers heard before his private front
as he lands place with notables.
We call this tribute in a nutshell,
a miracle of entertainment.

Speaking of beaus sartorial,
perplexed young girl hands laugh to lovewise.
I am a lovely, irresistible girl
of seventeen, with wondrous witching orbs.
Why do I blaze in my intangibles
like any mandolin romantic,
you, stable as the sterling?

Wanted

Expert experiences black on white
by men who are all white from the midriff
to the arches through the lowest joints.
We train you in accepted imagery,
the sights of love, and other popular sports,
and keep your eyes peeled for the gems of gab.
Diction or fact, it's all one to the larynx,
that is, one without gentile deformations.

The applicant is to be oriented,
a hustler from his collarbutton up,
upright and spry, a snotshooter who spares
no words or pleasant whispers of address.
Report to us at once with sample pomp
and testimonies of urbanity.

Also a man to master mockery,
a spotlighter with strong intentions.

Superproduction

St. Louis songbirds in Atlanta.
Just a minute. This is romance.
Enter Nancy, picking daisies.
Plughole sounds on the verandah.
All under the bedsheets rise.
The eyes thaw open and detect.

With the change in weather,
exposed and cooped in cold,
Nancy solicits your attention.
Nancy lies finished and deceived,
a sight to make your eyes fail
in the heated rooms, poisoned
by Rudolf's talcum manner.
Now love is slain, and the well-groomed
lover is wanted in seven states.
Again perfidy clicks like a billiard ball
and bounds from unexpected cushions.
Nancy's beloved body travels
the long way in a silent box,
unscented, unattended
by rhythmical gloved gentlemen.

Voices demand a happy ending.
Let her find more comfortable quarters,
then, through any heated savior.

Revue

They say in dreams they have a peetweet's view
of happy matters, but around them
and ahead stand fixtures of morality.
They scan these properties for some design
with a macabre elegant complexion,
but merely turn the screws of introspection;
turn and pick a ragtime on the strings,
and drink a soda to a better day,
when to a maiden's heart, the ace of wits,
calligrapher and creeping microskeptic,
equipped like tourists with a wordly light,
will sing the blues of a gregarian.

Hi Ho the Merio. Fashion decrees
shaved jawbones for established gents,
and sees them stripped to animal devotions,
swim in oceanic notions.

Leviathan and bulk of melancholy,
shine with us in miserable motions.

Impressions

The eyes are centered here
on this assumptive face,
with flowers by her cheek,
a moment as the eyes near
for the sight of that fraction,
only her eyes!

An uncle tips his high hat
and escorts her. Is it Sunday
that he bares his bright skull,
playing the uncle with all his flesh,
or just a fop's way on the avenue,
meeting skull with skull?

The merchant, Fagus, on her other side,
considers, leaves his name
and message on a card:
"Collect my follies in a vase.
Just a bouquet from an admirer."

The uncle and the lady time their strides,
and Fagus picks his way to comfort.

Little mood is to be gathered
from these sheepskin faces,
drumtight and wandering,
unless as primitive,
I move my bulk no nearer,
(brideless light affair)
but pass them with retentive eyes,
manifest and lonely.

Dolce Padre and Ephebus

Heavenly father,
learn that this commanding
young head which outshines
its antecedents, magnificent
and mortal compound on a tower, burns
with the cautery of affection.

And therefore, Master, flash
and magnify the canons
of perfection: in an ankle,
in the waistline, in the private
morals of this lady, holding
before our eyes, with wits divided,
an abstract of every man's spring.

(Our lord takes his experience
with amplitudes of fowl and fruit,
and lets the worm cover his slips,
and strip the pickings, even the thorn.)
        To which the young man:
"That atomweight of hawthorn,
of which you know, hold,

father, and do not blow
it off the point of concept,
for the masterweights of spring
equate like jewels."

The Founding of New Hampshire

A slender plank above a waterhole,
planted on end to meet my wants,
let me hear it whisper in the stock
or sway a hair's breadth and out it comes.
Another stake driven in and wellshaved
points against the light from the layout,
                              poor pointing.
The maple fits upon the joist like a flower,
                         a picked beam,
a great wood to plane and saw.
I tell my wife the walls are up,
the strips nailed at snug right angles,
                     the floors are oiled.
The Yankee poles are almost columns.

Braced against a gloomy magnitude,
I loiter civil on my soles and buffetted,
killing time in these traditions.
Are the woodsmells getting sweeter,
or the broker working at my back,
so that all the concord in the timber
can not warm this house?

Extracts from a Private Life

1

Your second cousin, an obscure cigar maker from Smyrna,
impresses me with tom thumb news.
The words are blunt and throw a sour limelight.
He regrets the way your eye
                            gluts on the dancing girls
like an oyster in the head of Bacchus.

But his hands too explore this woman's calf,
his hide lights up above her loincloth
                            like a white spark by an epitaph.

2

Witnessed the atom of the element boron
at zero in a classic crucible —

the sub-beat of the summer's metronome
(the organheat of Fez prefigured by
a salved cosmopolis of koranmen)

the birdclef of Manhattan Limited
(a mudhen in a shooting gallery).

Picked up the signet of these hanging contras,
and baled in words.
                    The pince-nez spied
across the astral valance in straight mercurial lines.

3

My houselights thunder like a tungsten pigeon,
and a leafshadow takes cover in the wainscot
                    like a hound.
I lock my doors against the beastly draughts.

The light above the chessmen spoke:
I am Avalokiteshvara Matsyendranatha, Lord of Fishes.
Your haunches shall be buried tomorrow by finished skeptics,
like big god pater Jove magnificent.

4

My wants are like the sparrows of a shepherd,
bony and dark on every shoulder,
                    and the hair and thumbs,
flying in a beautiful electric order.

Here I catch the pulse in my ear
                    trot out like a horse on asphalt,
or the watch under my pillow
                    singing like Venetian glass.

5

The bitterness are in these eyes
which can not bear the sight of a woman
because they are crowned
                    with an earthy taste,
because the candelabra of the mind
                    is black and cleancut.

Salts black and basic,
                    go the way
of wine and women into lyric matters.

6

Lay down the book, and match your wits
                    against this bird (when day
breaks) and your lover's broken teeth
before they sink you like the quips of Jesus.

Orphean Lost

The oakboughs of the cottagers
descend, my lover,
with the bestial evening.
The shadows of their swelled trunks
crush the frugal herb.
The heights lag
and perish in a blue vacuum.

And I, my lover,
skirt the cottages,
the eternal hearths and gloom,
to animate the ideal
with internal passion.

Fluteplayers from Finmarken

How keen the nights were,
Svensen.
Not a star out,
not a beat of emotion
in the humming snowhull.
(Now and then an awful swandive.)

It seemed ordained then that
my feet slip on the seal bones
and my head come down suddenly
over a simple rock-cistvaen,
grief-stricken and archwise.
Thereon were stamped
the figures of the noble women
I had followed with my closed eyes
out to the central blubber
of the waters.

(There is not a pigeon
or a bee in sight.
My eyes are shut now,
and my pulse dead as a rock.)

The Swedish mate says he recalls
this fungoid program of the mind and matter,
where the abstract signals to the abstract,
and the mind directs a final white lens
on the spewing of the waterworm
and the wings of the midsea.

It was not clear what I was after
in this stunted flora
and husky worldcold
until the other flutes arrived:
four masters musing
from one polar qualm to another.

Unswerving Marine

This is in the wind:
that an old seaman
                    paces the planks again
as his weedy hull parts
                    the saltseries inaudibly.
What ho! She carries full sails
And the chant of the grog-quaffers
                            in an important manner.
But there is no port
and the wind is distracted
                    from her simple stern
like the mind.
Continuously the undefined plane
                            emerges
in the form of a ship,
her nose speeding in the brine-ellipsis,
routing the shads and alewives
                            from her shaping way.
And the wind
and the mind sustain her
                    and there is really
no step upon the gangway,
nothing but the saltdeposits
                    of the open.

Before You

Before you is Corinth—
once a pedestal for wrestlers
in classical shorts.
What method in their manner!
Shall we say the gods
with lights behind us
have broken wind
in a changing system?
Yesterday behind the olive boughs
they too were lucid.
Send us again, O gods,
peppers and poppyseed,
porphyry and white cocks.

After a thousand years
Saint Casper said: Behold
the apple blossoms of the new world,
the early grapes,
the young man's cartograph
on which appears an arrow
pointed north to heaven.
There the gentle still idealize,
the heart is lighter.
And the good Cross is attended.

But we pass obscurely
from post to sleep,
opening the constructions
of the virtuous and loghouse
Puritans of Massachusetts.
They planted radishes
and hailed the Savior
spreading His alarming
feathers over the pickets.

A country house in April
after a thousand years.
Poor headpiece,
you are unhappy.
Buy yourself some alcohol for winter
and a squirrel rifle for Sunday morning.
You too will juggle
rabbits, eggs, bananas—
physical and resolute.

Tumblers in the nebula,
is not every man
his own host?

Revue

FROM SINAI TO KILLARNEY, a comic burst,
with other harmonies and egopedes,
wherein are found the shamrock and the redhead,
and that beloved disjoint of merry woman,
lovely McCohen herself, the Lark.
Behind the baritone is love's own cottage
where the misfits look out on the health
and blossomtime of Plymouth Rock.

McCohen smiled. "What eyes," lamented Bob,
"their shadowboxing interests me."

"Will she speak in orphic with the eyes
of insight and the plasma of elation?
Or the voice of analytic hesitation?
For her family is but an egg.
The myth and good form leave her.
                    Look,
they fly like the Pacific golden plover,
and laughter follows like a dying whale."

Death Song

Young utopia of spring-greens,
hello,
        light the towers
of the Whiskey King.
Behold the mints and comics of the season,
as the tempers light our reason
with penumbra and with chroma.

The Pollys in the Tenderloin
size up the town and vocalize.
The wise guy plucks a banjo string
for Polly's Irish eyes.

Only the fathers of the state
have public welfare up their sleeves.
Big-hearted Dick lays down the law,
and trots around in chevron weaves,
with dividends from patron markets,
picking his manner from the facts
of God, the flying American.

Sylvia

Trot out the negro singers, ladies, clowns
and athletes to extol the morning.
Let the senator take out his dogs
to swim, and watch the sliding of the lake
below the smooth urns, ships cantabile
and oceanic near the stratospheric.

The fair man in the public eye has read
the private life of simple Jesus,
Casuist and Undertaker of the West.
Sylvia hails him from a torpedo roadster.

He clears his title to her loins,
gets shaved and trimmed in the venereal parlors,
where he rakes in on the wheel of love,
his standing polished like a dental mirror,
his old age lit up like a christmas tree.

Salons

Clear me with this master music when
the coryphee skips on the bright oak, when
the clouds depress me like the lower keys,
and penitentially the rib bones throb.
This drama sets the clocks of epigram.

The grave salons with lines of peridot
in the interior and cairngorm pomp,
attest refinements of the clavichord.

The pieces are the will of shadows, and
the person in the polished doorway feels
the dark mask of his chamber sentiments.

These are the privacies behind the mask,
but they are not the manners of a boy
who blows his French horn, smiles at twelve o'clock,
and sips the old port from the hostess' shoe.

This etiquette is stranger than those fats
of fellowship, which turn the apricot
liqueur and absinthe into innocence,
the bottles into happy unities
among its pie-eyed sobbing hooligans.

The Athletes

A technical display.
You bought a perfume bottle
and a Chinese shawl.
Susannah set a headstone in St. Paul.

I'm inside waiting for a surprise
I'm in love with the girl on the Wabash
I'm alone with a hand in my hand
and a pair of wonderful eyes.

But you're blue
you have to speak
you want to do
you want to see
the sights obscure you
the facts secure you.

The Maine sails out to sea.
The undertaker drives to Hartford.

Somebody has to drive the spikes
pitch the gears

oil the cams
somebody has to kill the whiskey
somebody has to speak.

Yesterday the ducks flew in a mackerel sky.
You had the allotropes of vision,
something historical at the controls of North
America, heavyweight and metaphorical.

What are the facts?
They swept the city hall today.
They set the lathe dogs
trimmed the tool posts
scraped the bearings
shellacked the knots.
They set the capital
upon the shaft.
What are the facts?

Amulet

But you are ideal,
O figurette,
and cool as camphor.
You wander formal
in an ice-green panelette.

The small blue eyes
are set in jadework.
And your hand stings
like a drop of witch-hazel.

Bless the white throat
of this lady
drinking clabber milk
at a buffet lunch.

Song

Turning as from an instrument
the faces open like a choir,
shining from the pillars
in quadragesimal sentiment.

The eyes are folded and assume
a coronation music.
One by one the fluent breaths
respond in the gloom.

Briefly the eyes uphold
their warm heroic acclamations.
Briefly the voices touch;
the eyes grow cold.

Sealight

After the jostling on canal streets
and the orchids blowing in the windows
I work in cut glass and majolica,
and hear the plectrum of the angels.

My thoughts keep dwelling on the littoral,
where china clocks tick in the cold shells
and the weeds slide in the equinox.

The night is cold for love.
We favor the chorus
and the antistrophe of the sealight.

Handel

The piccolo of heaven
climbed the scales.
A blue cusp sank
like gauze.
The book of dawn
fell open on my brow,
a chronicle of the eternal virgin
graciously held
by archimandrite hands.
I saw divisions like the zodiac,
and from the blue
the ice-light of an afternoon.

Paraguay

In the early hours the lovebirds
colonized the palm.

We were looking for a totem.
Finding nothing
but the Indian smells,
we booked the next boat to Janeiro.

On the east coast,
when the sun deflects the falcons
from their sea-positions,
we found a blessed frère
with no cathedral
but the daisies in May,
living on milk and wafers,
with the cross in one hand
and the anatomy of sorrow in the other.

Frankfort and Bethlehem

8/10

This postcard has the Christmas
spirit with its Lutheran
steeple between the hills
its cow fence and its fir tree
and a dirt farm in Thuringia.

Bright star, unto you
is born this day
a grub in the addle.

Paris

9/8

A Bohemian idea
of a plankwalk to the sea,
a smoked salmon on a line,
a ball of packing twine...
everything in eggs and cubes
as effortless and helpless
as if waiting for a corpse
with Jockey Club and heliotrope.

Here comes the bride
with kewpie blue eyes
and a lighted brassiere.
It's a gay life.

Quote me as a humorist
with a gardenia
in my cutaway.

Foyer, The Orpheum

12/10

During the water movement
of the French horns
and the lovelace of a violin
a wire from my girl. She says
"I love you but I need a deposit."
Even the ventriloquist's dummy laughed
after we combed his pretty red hair
and set him on his tricycle.

The Professor   Do you know the story of Lou?
She was a lonely little gal
with the love in her eyes
and Mr. H. H. at the ivories.
And she was happy (honest to God).
In the season of Romain effects
and synthetic American lights
she drove into a Western suburb
in a seven-bearing gull-line Suiza,
rolling her kleig eyes
like revolving doors.

Animal Cartoons	Whereupon the jackass full of animal gas floated blissfully into the dance of the seven veils.
Professor	Poor Lou in the climax to the Latin scene gave up the fareast of the imagination for seven rooms in Arkansas.
Lou	I have that funny feeling. It must be love.
Mr. Rakosi	Nothing so marks the copulative man as a corkscrew and a bottle opener.
Lou	Feel my pulse, please. Can it be the tropics?
Mr. Rakosi	Yes, I have a joking knowledge of many topics. It's the moonlight if you insist. Your lips are difficult to resist. Pardon me while I go to sleep.
Lou	You're so deep. Why don't you talk in English?

V's Dummy	I could almost weep. Are you my father?
Ventriloquist	That's my affair. Do you swear to uphold the constitution?
Dummy	On my wax banana. What the hell's going on here? I smell Pittsburgh.
Ventriloquist	It's a muscle dance it's sheet music piano tremoloing Benny Rubin Alabama chicken hop.
Porter	Can't be bothered now happy breeches. I'll be seein ya. Pick me out a nice jail.
Tom Nelson	Could you stand an old man to a cup of coffee? It's hard walking with this silver septum in my nose.
	Tom Nelson from the Old Royal buck and wing man.

A Journey Away

1

The wayfarer met the passerby
in death's champaign of flowers.
As the lint blew through their skulls
they spoke discreetly of the next world,
of the slobland to the left
the awful coprolite above.
The words were impressive and muted.
Suddenly the one preoccupied
with his obsolete luetic eyeball
made a meaningless aside
in keeping with the serious scene.

2

I dreamed last night
that I was married.
I was scared, the woman
being very young, with green
stones in her garter.

She looked upon me wistfully
                    and said:

I was a taxi dancer
with a sweetheart on a fishing smack.
I perceive by these pains
that I am condemned to die.

From Okeanos sprang her hot breath.
Her image is an ancient blue glass,
                              so subtle.
It reminded me
of one I had not seduced.
She was brushing out her hair
before the mirror.
I should have been arranging
the white poppies in the window
with the coriander.

3

You were travelling through Delos
when the end came.

On the esplanade at Cannes
the awnings suddenly
went black before me.
I was carried to the belvedere
of Villa Policastro.
In the evening, dearly beloved,
in the sight of blood and bandages
I lay there like a dressed fowl.
On a marble seat above the Ligurian
another evening.

An ideal
like a canary
singing in the dark
for appleseed and barley.

Something from the laurel,
                    a tiny arsis.

        4

Above the fireplace
the portrait of an old man
with a fowling piece
and period whiskers.
Sir William Cavendish
6th Bart. and brevet-major
11th Hussars.
                    Crest
and shield: a demi-man
affronté in armor,
the helmet adorned
with three feathers,
holding in the dexter
hand a scimitar.
Two miner's picks.
Omne Solum Forti Patria.

5

We climbed the stairs,
the white dress flowing
from the lady's sides.
She turned the pottery lamp.
How shall I wear you,
center crown stone, great
blue solitaire of sentiment?
They will say I am Jewish.

She took my hand and pointed out
the men's shops with terrazzo floors,
the city desks, the shoe windows,
the Carlton waiters with a canapé
of coral lobster, 666 for colds
and fevers, the suburban shore drive,
the old man hammering in the doll shop.

So light the room, like air
about a willow branch.
A glass stands on the golden table.
Prints of St. Marks, The Bargello,
Mme. Lebrun and Her Daughters.
A glass vase with a spinning stem.

"This is my daughter Sue"
and sat adamic as with jug
and towel for a painter.

A young girl's study. Lace.
And nimbus from the north.
She played a classical pianoforte
clef-wandering sweet pinna tremolo
a Chippendale in a dominoes etude:
the Bird pirriko pirriko prrrk
      ia ia
the leghorn rustling in the brush
the creek between the rockshelves
Nancy with a bunch of wet grapes.

6

A light in the morning
crystallized upon the crest
entranced the virgin.
There the fawn stood
hunted, bated, sensitized
and sainfoin breath,
being unknown to himself
a cornea of light.

7

Sea-kin,
we have broken away.
Our hearts are grounded

in the waterways.
Our butts foam
in the current like a keel.
We pray you,
let your wings blaze
in the sterling course.

8

The black arena bull bleeds in the neck.
The ladies are gone. I throw a rose
upon the black loins. Tomorrow another
bull fight and the gall irk of cafard and sceptic.

Keep the whisky from me.

9

One o'clock. A rainy night.
The sea air darkens on the wheelhouse.
The binnacle glows.
                    "Ho there! Ho!"
The Frisco Cross, a twin-screw tanker
burns in the hull.
                    "Who are you?"
A dry face. The chronometer tilts.
"All lights burning brightly, Sir." Ist Ruhe.

Parades

Return, sweet ladies, in aplomb and apostolic passage
    with streamers blown before our patronage.

    Preceded by the favored birds,
the clouds escort you with an ancient program.

This is but the English of a lonely sharp-eyed one
    who weeps a moment
                        in adoration.

African Theme, Needlework, etc.

1

One must have sullen wits to foot the jungle
like another darkness because of heimweh
and an air spiced with big fruit.
The bamboos shiver and the tattooed bird
caws to the rose-chafer in the moon.
It's mumbo-jumbo banging a tom-tom, his black
feet straggling in the thrum of oil palms.
Ivory hunters with a tree mask
come up the river. Apes, apes.
In the tiger country beyond the grain
the black one rolls her pubes.
The continent is waterbound and one
outside the singer in the shack,
and Sambo, fat cigar in heaven, chucks
the white dice gravely with a black crow.

2

Over the fan-tan table and the tea and noodles
one admires the return to Lisbon
of the navigator on the needlework,
who sailed the Hansa routes with linen,
point-lace, hardware, and camphor wood,
bearing private letters from the Augsburg
bankers, the owners of the ships of Ghent.
Now with his own slave and a clock
he stands under one sail, looking home.
Before him coral, geese, boats,
and an unknown woman under a palm
with strawberries charmingly out of proportion.
                    And a photograph
of table service, bright
as on the day it came from the factory.

The Islands

In the salt warp
was the plasma
in the springhead
and the sulphurous
                    water.
Jupiter the sire hawk
flew through Athens.
Then the Greeks sang,
the wings turned through
the light turned through
the palm. We sat upon a
stone with happy records.
Athens the Greek hawk
was no parakeet.

But in the dense scopes
they are shipping
kelp and sulphur
through the islands.
                  My master
has been perfumed Christian
and fishes in the reefs

with ancient weights —
or sometimes wanders
an apocryphal white goat.

Light the filaments.
The image is in ancient
                    ink.

Consider Hrothgar the wandering scop
heartrover among your fathers
kept his sails upon the North Sea
with a load of deer hides and bird feathers
2000 tods of whalebone for the Danes.

(Oilburn of sentiment)

Or Saracen physicians
under a pecan tree,
busy with the heart.

(This also burns
                    Damascus)

Dearly beloved folksounds,
fellow agents,
kurion onoma yolkbearers,
the strangeness
is my insulator
but my heart is sound.

Happy New Year

A little river steamer from the tariff frontiers,
twelve cabins, and a white light on the masthead,
with its house flag and a freeboard of 6", boys
running with mates' receipts and bills of lading,
kilderkin imperial kegs and stingo firkins.

Great turbo-electric ocean liner, fire insured,
with circulating ice water swift for the belly—
foreign mail, the anchor hook, reporters,
customs men, the mail boat and the nova.

The Memoirs

A cutter risen from the mollusks, it is a god
with a god carved on the stempiece
arriving in Detroit with Jesuits,
feluccas, pinnaces and brigantines,
the mainsail hauled out on a little tackle.

Here cometh what hath broken your legs...
the king of France, the Secretary for the Latin
Tongue, the Lord High Butler of England
with coronation jewels, and the chandlers.

They have broken me for the last time.
I spit on them al.
They lie on the high poop al the night
with open eye, with wenches, singing
in radium like Chaucer and the smale fowles.

A sail in Atlantis in the morning, a Sappho
of a sloop slapping the buss ship London
white and anchored as a living clam.
Michigan freshwater walnut trees.
The memoirs/
                canvas, cable, chain, tar, paint.

Good Prose

A yellow feather
of a note

delighted bounding
canary birdcry

Up, my Norwich,
spit the bitter

gravel out,
throw out the little

ball in midair.
Unlike "stymphalian

birds that eat up
the fruit," this male

surveys his cuttlebone
of Mediterranean

his biscuit and his seed
from a trapeze bar

with wetting waxy
claws.
      Come,
           my
Lancashire Coppy,
the sun lights up

the lettuce leaf
between the bars.

Sappho

steps out
from a lily

in the clear
bearing a quince

creator
calling

the ships out,
radiant

in cloth
and water

like a daisy
in the hand.

But what
is memory
among women?

She lifts
the linen

and speaks.
The ships

are radiant.
Man rises

from the kiss
and answers yes.

The Classics

The girls
wear ear rings

on the water
silver beaten

with a punch
the carved end

striking out
two flowers.

This day
the young

men, sternum
in the water,

swim below
the cutter races.

Women used to
pass into the

public buildings
with a blue jug

on their heads
and stand

like statues
with the noses

knocked off,
commemorating

the signing
of the peace.

The Gnat

Winter and wind,
the whole age

is an afternoon
around the house

a little snow
a sea blizzard

a yard clover
a lucky house

anabasis
for edelweiss

Six rivers
and six wenches

the twelve
victories.

Greetings.

Carl Rakosi

The Wedding

Under this Luxemburg of heaven
"upright capstan
                    small eagles—
port of N.Y."

gilders, stampers, pen makers, goldbeaters,

fear of thunder
        speed
    the whore
        indifference
    son
        glioma
    water
        burial

Tammany, McCoy,
the bronze doors of the Guarantee Trust,
the copper spandrels

orangerie and game room,
Old English tall twisted
stem engraved goblets

Royal Copenhagen porcelain,
mutton fat jade Chien Lung
                              bowl

a toilet bottle
                amethyst
stopper & a monogram shield

Peeled from its mesentery
the heart was extracted
on a board washing and beating

between the two gold vases of Bermuda lilies

an actborn egg shape
twisted like Ugolino

broken Sunday memories
a multiplication of pianos
touch ideal and invitation

St. Chrysostom's carillon-
carilloneur—between
the organ and the white gown

One sea water, one circulatory system
of man observing his magnificent urea,
and the red hair—
                    walks in bride's fear.

Men on Yachts

After the bath she touched her hair
with Orange Leaf and smiled.

Henry is gone. Who are you?

Fumous ashwood stationary violins
all night made bright da capo
constant as specific gravity.
So the umbrellas were put away.

We were together on yachts and beaches,
breakfasts on the ocean,
taxis through the Brandenburger Tor.

Along the Danube
                    onion stew and cart hack,
sheep under the Carpathians,
the cheese upon the rack.
The heifers licked their noses.

                    Along the Boston limited
commercial service.

The table in the boarding house
was cleared, the cloth folded.
The rooms contained a few flowers,
chocolate boxes, women,
a laundry bag,
the lipstick on the dresser.

The men fled military service in the Empire.

The Lobster

to W. Carlos Williams

Eastern Sea, 100 fathoms,
green sand, pebbles,
broken shells.

Off Suno Saki, 60 fathoms,
gray sand, pebbles,
bubbles rising.

Plasma-bearer
and slow-
motion benthos!

The fishery vessel Ion drops
anchor here collecting
plankton smears and fauna.

Plasma-bearer, visible sea
purge, sponge and kelpleaf,
Halicystus the Sea Bottle

resembles emeralds
and is the largest
cell in the world.

Young sea-horse
Hippocampus twenty
minutes old—

nobody has ever
seen this marine
freak blink.

It radiates on
terminal vertebrae
a comb of twenty

upright spines
and curls
its rocky tail.

Saltflush lobster
bull encrusted swims
backwards from the rock.

The Beasts

1

Fresh mollusk morning puts a foot
out from its bivalve.
Behind us skeleton of sea-
cucumber, microscopic
buttons, tables, plates, wheels
and anchors in its skin.

A hydroid, wrasse in hundreds,
the anchovy, the horse mussel,
blue sturgeon, spiny cockle,
underwater fairy palm expanding.

Before us land,
the goat in open field.
The milk is marketed.
Attend our table.

For the evening is the city's
like a shell forced open
and the foreign matter
shining sea-forced pearl.

The great names, like the sand,
the fluorspar and the soda ash
make a blue
              aventurine glass
for this city

that as you enter, Weep
it says at either panel
of the door and rises
from the base in one piece,
one of two stone figures
with her head bowed.
And above, a lion rampant
on his hind feet, royally
clawing, tail whipped up.

This way the little banjo
music enters the hotel.

This way the channeled ceiling
luminaires
              of the National
Bank of Commerce
metal finish crystal ground floor
and small grilled windows,
the banking hours.

Lamp
     with goddess
holding
     twin fish,
ivory carved Japanese lady,
hands crossed over breast,
holding on her head
the electric bulbs
and batik lamp shade.

   2

Immigrants from Lodz
in a furnished room
close to the stores.
Porcelain pitcher,
bath and hand towels
on the bed rails.

A new sign goes
into the window *Smocking
Hemstitching,   Rhinestone
          Setting*

Come, great city

                    petroleum oil,
domestic sulphite, Old Paper,
Newsroll Contract, short wool,
kip, Ohio & Pa. fleeces,
fine up-river rubber,
tank plates, wire nails,
China wood oil, mason's lime,
pine roofers, spruce lath,
basket-fired Japan tea,
the white Singapore pepper,
burlap, Newfoundland cod.

At least we'll have a snack.
The city has full powers of
attorney to protect its friends.

One hour from here
                    a loggia
above the pepper trees,
a tiny cascade and vines
above the bath house,
men and women driving
on the fairway, laughing,
surrounded by Galloway
pottery, garden furniture
and white daisies.

3

When the light sprang from the sea, blowing,
the window sintered and blew like Venus
on my younger brother.

Tenderness and the idea
caught one like an animal
in night photography.

Contested between two responsibilities
like a gizzard thrown to two dogs,
judging between two faiths
I saw the city

changed, set up like laboratory
glassware, like amines of herring brine,
the malic acid of the sea buckthorn,
glass-enclosed prescription balance
steel and agate, Fabrik Köln

a physics clear as alcohol,
La Vita Nuova, I hardly knew.

Creditors dined at the Cliquot Club.
They read the papers, trade changed.
Their horses died, the big-bellied.
Their dogs slept in the steam heat.

In an ambulance with modest
glass doors and a silver cross

a surgeon, delicate nickel-plate
instruments are laid on trays

illuminated on the operating table

                    naked glassblowers,
gunsmiths, barbers, clerks, importers,
old men from hotels, pink and tailored.
Naphthasmelling Irish priests.
Cravat-and-boy face of the movie usher.
Frankel, Shmulik, Old Country watchmakers.

Then a white horse in the park.
Cigars and politics.
The city wrapped in cellophane.

The Poem

It is orchids
blowing in
the windows

to the night
the stairways
the canals

I work in cut
glass
and majolica

and hear
the plectrum
of the angels

blowing
chorus chorus
my thoughts

keep dwelling
on the littoral
the cold

shells, China
Cold is the gut

and beast
   the living one.

National Winter Garden Shamrock

The blazing crocus
musical review form-
ation brings down
          the house
Arms linked
the chorus girls
powdered and smiling
climb into a bandbox
with a love song
in which Ireland
is green as wallpaper
and lassies carry
old-fashioned
romantic baskets
on the Emerald Isles.

The Black Crow

One must have sullen wits
to foot the jungle
like another darkness
because of heimweh
and an air spiced
with big fruit. Four
spooky winds tackle
one's knees like a swoon.
The bamboos shiver
and the tattooed bird caws
to the rose-chafer in the moon.
Now though one's black feet
straggle in the thrum
of oil palms, mumbo-jumbo
bangs a tom-tom.

The continent is waterbound
and one outside the singer
in the shack. And Sambo,
fat cigar in heaven,
chucks the white dice
gravely with a black crow.

Country People Never Learn

They are the same everywhere.
This one driving
his cart along the Danube,
why should he give up
his good sheep
and his open fields
and the sight of goats
on the Carpathians
for a strange war
in a strange land?

To My First Born

I felt your foot below your mother's breast
and said, "I am your provider,
let us get to know each other.
You have made me write a poem
and wake the neighbors with my shouting
until they cry, 'What does he
think he is, the god of love?'"

Pike-Eater's Song

The hours
come
into the city,

horses breathing
on a sprig
and fishermen

with ale glass
in a window
singing Old Rose.

The People

O you in whom distrust lies under
    like a gallstone
and desire grows up aching
    like a sharp tooth,
courage rises over all
    because it is your heart
and knows no high airs or aloofness.

When I was young
and my moods stood between us,
you made me feel lonely.

Now I plant myself
in the middle of the street
and swear I shall never leave you,
for you stand between me and my moods.

To the Non-Political Citizen

Every man is entitled to his anger.
It's in the Constitution.
Every man is also entitled
to his own opinion and his own death,
his own malice and his own villainy.

But you spend too much time goosing.
You choose your words too carefully
and are afraid of being called agitator.

When will you become indignant
and declare yourself
against the wrongs of the people?

To a Collie Pup

The way you look up at me
with a saint in each eye
one would think I never fed you
and that I was just a convenience
to take you walking.

Why you are hardly old enough
to know the difference
between your own tail and a shadow,
yet you chase birds and chickens
and steal bread from the neighbor's trashcans.

How is it that you play with my shoelace
and understand so well how to love me?

For this you shall have
the key to my bedroom.

Declaration

I shall put my purity away now
and find my art in other men
before I end up like a taper
in the bedroom of an old maid.

I am tired of wearing out my seat
regretting I was not Shakespeare

and trying to make my reading
approach an age like memory
a mother's face, restoring dimly
here a tooth and here a smile

or plucking a lute
and singing a madrigal.

This is no time to be looking backward.
I am for public action and public hate
and I am impatient to declare myself.

To an Anti-Semite

So you fought for the Jews
in the last war
and have become a patriot again!

Why you thick-skulled liar
as impossible to offend
as to trust with an order,

you were never within
three thousand miles
of the front.

You fought the war
in Camp McKinley,
cleaning stables

and stealing out
into the moonlight
with the kitchen maids.

And now I find you
trying to drive the Jews
and Communists out of America!

Dedication

to the house
and its white linen,

to the chubb, his guts out,
the grass from his throat
and fresh herbs in his belly,

to the draper's English
whose sincerity is like a horse
and rider on a sanded path,

to Izaac Walton's English
sounding like the small bell
of the knife-grinder,

to the trout carved in the table
of the little fishing-house
which gives greenwood to the water.

Good tongue to you all
who like the chubb
are tied with splinters.

APPENDIX

Unpublished, Never Completed, and Revised Poems

Travels Among the Yakahulas

Trot out the circus barkers, ladies, clowns,
and athletes to extol the fleshpoints of the morning.
Call them Fire on the Angels' Butts,
and spot the tealeaf figure of the lake
below the smooth urns, ships cantabile,
the oceanic native drum of clouds.

He, Oswald, climbs upon the rocks to read
the private life of simple slippery Jesus.
Katinka hails him from a dashing roadster,
then joins the daughters of the clean republic.

We leave him polished like a dental mirror,
show him waiting on her freckled loins,
a strategist in the venereal parlors
where he rakes in on the wheel of love,
his old age lit up like a Christmas tree.

A *Predilection*

My Venice: modern Europe and Siam
And Egypt in San Marco's scuff of heels;
Typewriters strumming on the diaphragm
In Canaletto's dark canals, —

Eyes the colors of dragonflies,
And violet eyes, o Yankee spleen,
Where the Adriatic accompanies
The song of the sewing-machine!

Equations

The tree and the stone are the only Nordics.

MacLeish is at bottom academic like Tate and Winters. The difference is he has attached himself like a sucker fish to Eliot and been towed along. Tate's criticism too has this sucker organ. MacLeish's "Open Letter to the Young Men of Wall St." in the Sat. Review of Lit. shows the pusillanimous rhetoric that is the nerve of his style. The better he writes, the more evident it becomes that he is not an original, as his hosts were.

In poetry one should not wait until one knows what one believes.

The results of suspending subtlety in art for ten years would be illuminating. I offer in the place of this dandy: (1) drive; (2) firm, not insinuating, contrasts; (3) a purification of vocabulary, vide Marianne Moore; (4) the electric shorthand of Cocteau and of Zukofsky in sections of "A"; (5) the enlargement of one's perceptions of new physical materials; (6) the suspension of stylistic disguise, chatter and play until one's personality really talks. One observes with respect this constant effort in Williams. And the result of all this would be a fresh

focus and exercise of language. No seductions and in-
sincerity, no attenuations. What a day! One could cel-
ebrate with Blake. Finally one would forget to look what
position Eliot takes.

The heavy rain drove the little donkey under a bush.
But his butt was exposed. When he moved forward, the
water fell into his eyes. So he moved back and stood
stolid. The rain made his belly stand out dark and his
legs scrawny and high-pegged. I could imagine a Sicil-
ian grape-gatherer kissing the donkey for his frankness.
A half hour later when I returned, he was picking at the
grass, unaware of the rain. He was equally frank but in
a different way. No one but an expert could have put
the donkey directly in front of the ferns.

A strange rose-colored butterfly on a picket. I have never
seen such a hypnotic one. As I come close I see it is not
a butterfly but a girl's bow. Damnation, this is the fa-
mous eosin dye, so called because it resembles the dawn.
It is often used to color wool and to sensitize photo-
graphic plates to the colors in the spectrum which the
human eye sees best. It annoys me that I can not com-
pare the temper of its discoverer and the nature of his
satisfaction with the emotional effects of a successful
phrase.

In moments of weakness one makes resolutions. In reso-
lution one's desire has stratified, one has already lost
some personality. And in one's strength one becomes
one's own opponent—a unit engine.

The Beasts
[Reconstruction]

1

Fresh mollusk morning puts a foot
out from its bivalve.
Behind us skeleton of sea
cucumber, microscopic
buttons, tables, plates, wheels
and anchors in its skin.

A hydroid, wrasse in hundreds,
the anchovy, the horse mussel,
blue sturgeon, spiny cockle,
underwater fairy palm expanding.

Before us land,
the goat in open field.
The milk is marketed.
Attend our table.

For the evening is the city's
like a shell forced open
and the foreign matter
shining sea forced pearl.

The great names like the sand,
the fluorspar and the soda ash
make a blue
                    aventurine glass
for this city

that as you enter, Weep
it says at either panel
of the door and rises
from the base in one piece,
one of two stone figures
with her head bowed.
And above, a lion rampant
on his hind feet, royally
clawing, tail whipped up.

This way the little banjo
music enters the hotel.

This way the channeled ceiling
luminaires
                of the National
Bank of Commerce
metal finish crystal ground floor
and small grilled windows,
the banking hours.

This private enterprise

orangerie and game room,
Old English tall twisted
stem engraved goblets

Royal Copenhagen porcelain,
mutton fat jade Chien Lung
                              bowl

a toilet bottle
                amethyst
stopper & a monogram shield

Lamp
        with goddess
holding
            twin fish,
ivory carved Japanese lady,
hands crossed over breast,
holding on her head
the electric bulbs
and batik lamp shade.

Immigrants from Lodz
in a furnished room
close to the stores.
Porcelain pitcher,
bath and hand towels
on the bed rails.

A new sign goes
into the window *Smocking
Hemstitching,   Rhinestone
                    Setting.*

Come, great city

                    petroleum oil,
domestic sulphite, Old Paper,
Newsroll Contract, short wool,
kip, Ohio & Pa. fleeces,
fine up river rubber,
tank plates, wire nails,
China wood oil, mason's lime,
pine roofers, spruce lath,
basket fired Japan tea,
the white Singapore pepper,
burlap, Newfoundland cod.

At least we'll have a snack.
This city has full powers of
attorney to protect its friends.

One hour from here
                    a loggia
above the pepper trees,
a tiny cascade and vines
above the bath house,

men and women driving
on the fairway, laughing,
surrounded by Galloway
pottery, garden furniture
and white daisies.

2

When the light sprang from the sea, blowing,
the window sintered and blew like Venus
on my younger brother.

Tenderness and the idea
caught one like an animal
in night photography.

Contested between two responsibilities
like a gizzard thrown to two dogs,
judging between two faiths
I saw the city

changed, set up like laboratory
glassware for amines of herring brine,
the malic acid of the sea buckthorn
glass enclosed prescription balance
steel and agate   Fabrik Koln

a physics clear as alcohol,
La Vita Nuova, I hardly knew.

Creditors dined at the Cliquot Club.
They read the papers, trade changed.
Their horses died, the big bellied.
Their dogs slept in the steam heat.

In an ambulance with modest
glass doors and a silver cross

a surgeon, delicate nickel plate
instruments are laid on trays

illuminated on the operating table.

          naked glassblowers,
gunsmiths, barbers, clerks, importers,
old men from hotels, pink and tailored,
naphthasmelling Irish priests.
Cravat and boy face of the movie usher.
Frankel, Shmulik, Old Country watchmakers.

Then a white horse in the park.
Cigars and politics.
The city wrapped in cellophane.

   3

After the bath she touched her hair
with Orange Leaf and smiled.

Henry is gone. Who are you?

Fumous ashwood stationary violins
all night made bright da capo
constant as specific gravity.
So the umbrellas were put away.

We were together on yachts and beaches,
breakfasts on the ocean,
taxis through the Brandenburger Tor.

Along the Danube
                    onion stew and cart hack,
sheep under the Carpathians,
the cheese upon the rack.
The heifers licked their noses.

                    Along the Boston limited
commercial service.

The table in the boarding house
was cleared, the cloth folded.
The rooms contained a few flowers,
chocolate boxes, women,
a laundry bag,
the lipstick on the dresser.

The men fled military service in the Empire.

The Old Men

You must be wondering how they got there,
old men with high-toned secretaries,
sitting in the cool of profit,
so respectable, so unlike a battlefield

perception without warmth,
craft without light,
growth without use.

How curious you must be about these indignant patriots
who designate you in the press as Red,
respectable important men unlike you
with your common touch, your great intimate encounters.

They bring you an old envy,
they breathe into you a subtle rapacity.

You must be wondering how they got there,
big shots with high-toned secretaries.

Heroes bought and sold
opinions paid for and delivered
Envy free with the subtle perfume of rapacity.

Heroes Bought and Sold

Let us voice our opinions in the peace
of respectability and labor without self-interest.

Let us admire the rich and cultivate rapacity.
Let us seek self-fulfillment also
in our virtues as they do in their possessions.

Let us be whimsical and well-bred
as others are implacable.
This will bring distinction to our family
and luster to our self-esteem.

Let us be condescending as others are condescending to us.
Let us stand aloof from popular movements, let us be different
Let us be critical of positive conviction
Let us be tentative as others are implacable

Let us be diffident & tender with the masses
but let us stand aloof from crowds.

Two words joined venally in the speech
of our people: life and property.

Let us have poets write
about their long-necks and their high-born air.

Let us be thankful for our aspirations
but observe a decent distance to them.

Life and property are joined already
in the language of the people

as *life* and *property* are joined
in the language of the law.

A Dollar is a Man's Best Friend

If the button-pushers with their high-toned secretaries
must refer to you contemptuously in the press as Red
it's only a reflection of rapacity.

If small-eyed poets, long necked, high-chested like swans,
prefer to go downstream in a silver mist,
it's of no consequence, let them go.
Let the indolent feathers and the tiny skulls go,
Good riddance to their high-born air.

But you without airs. You are the people. Red belongs to you
as much as to the sun and the vital organs of your enemies.

They make me think of small eyed carnivorous birds
rapaciously flying from the very nesthead of the state
with the vital organs of their victims hanging from their beaks.

We'll take these cats apart and see what makes them say
money talks.
"A dollar is a man's best friend"

If money talked I'd hate to hear what it had to say.
On second thought, I like this candor. No man can believe this.
To acknowledge so much is to say that one is not satisfied
with one's false face & wd. like to have something better.

The Legion

When Hirohito writes on New Year's, "Peaceful
is morning in the shrine garden";

when Mrs. Chamberlain in Westminster prays for peace
while Neville is in Berchtesgaden selling it;

when Mussolini's son observes, "One group of horsemen
gave me the impression of a budding rose
as the bombs fell in their midst."

When Hitler cries, "The shelling of Almeira
did more for peace than all the London discussions.
We do not want war, but we can not stand by
and see our great defenseless German people
delivered to the arrogance of Communists
and the cunning of the Jews."

When in my own land
I see the clown applauded
& the worker defiled

the serious public word hated
for it draws us to the people
& we do not wish to be drawn,
we are unaffectables, untouchables.

When in my own land
I see the crowd surround
and applaud the drunken clown

This zany is a specimen of the people
we the observers are also people
but we are cleaner,
we have more money & power
The others are amusing

Labor despised by its own leaders
strikers shot down & children scabbing for a lark
vigilantes drafted from the sons
in a hurry to be men

I yearn to blow, blow
the mouthpiece through the trumpet
in a piercing blast

To Pa Coughlin

Daladier, Hitler, Chamberlain, Mussolini......
once before my writing failed me
in the middle of my life, and I was helpless.
Now again it fails me before their names,
their villainy stinks so,

and I puke with anger,
turning my mirror to the wall, the glass
in which I dreamed of greatness.
That trick will not work again.
I see no poet in the glass now but a small
distrustful boy who cannot execute his claims.
No one shows him where his place is.
All the front seats and the balcony are taken.
Only standing room is left, a loneliness
where he can be original as he likes
and no one minds it if he feels distinguished.

Yes, I recognize the place and boy
but wish to notify my friends
that I am no longer at that address,

for I have seen division among workers
turned to frightful consequence.

Here, here is the true glass for a poet.

And so I claim the body of the boy
to bury not to honor, for he fought
for no cause and he leaves behind
no grieving relatives. His corpse is one
I shd. not like to see in a public place.

Surrealists (1930)

During the water movement of the French horns
and the lovelace of a violin
I had a wire from my girl which said
I love you but I need a deposit.
Even the ventriloquist's dummy laughed.

Did you say laugh? How about the moonlight,
which is difficult to resist, by which Salome,
animal cartoon ass, dances with her lovely ball?

How about the copulative man
with a corkscrew and a bottle opener?

I don't get you.
Why don't you talk in English?

You don't get me?
I have the blues, I have to tear.

But somebody has to drive the spikes,
pitch the gears, oil the cams.

Not me, brother! I'm inside waiting for a surprise,
I'm in love with the girl on the Wabash,
I'm alone with a hand in my hand
and a pair of wonderful eyes.

Well, somebody has to set the lathe dogs,
trim the tool posts, scrape the bearings,
somebody has to shellac the knots.

Wrong number, operator! I'm a humorist with a gardenia
in my cutaway, waiting for a corpse.

The city hall has to be swept once in a while.

Go away, brother, I'm a genius.
I have a responsibility to my public.

Say, could you stand an old man to a cup of coffee?

Listen, old man! I draw a sweet note out of myself
and have no time for other strangeness.

The Wedding

Between the two gold
vases of Bermuda lilies
go the egg shaped

feelings of a man
fearing son and whore,
feeling his heart

peeled from its mesentery
and washing and beating
on a board between the organ

and the bride's gown,
and his memory touched
with ideal and invitation.

The Status Quo

It is good to be here.
This city is a shell forced open
and the foreign matter shining sea-forced pearl.

But the people who made this city
out of sand and petroleum oil,
domestic sulphite, Old Paper,
Newsroll Contract, short wool,
kip, Ohio & Pa. fleeces,
fine up-river rubber,
tank plates, wire nails,
China wood oil, mason's lime,
pine roofers, spruce lath,
basket-fired Japan tea,
white Singapore pepper,
burlap, Newfoundland cod, etc.

the people who made it all,
weep, rising from their base
like a single stone figure
with head bowed,

for the city belongs to its creditors,
chairmen of boards dining at the Club,
the city belongs to its newspapers
and its lawyers,
and the makers of this great city
had better hold on to their testicles!

Poetry

When the light sprang from the sea, blowing,
the window sintered and blew like Venus,
revealing my tenderness

and discovering the many minds
and the many responsibilities

the way a night shot discovers
a beast drinking.

Ships

One o'clock. A rainy night.
The sea air darkens on the wheelhouse.
The binnacle glows.
      "Ho there, ho!"
The whole hull of *The Frisco Cross*,
a twin-screw tanker, lights up.
      "Who are you?"

A dry face. The chronometer tilts.
"All lights burning brightly, sir."

A little river steamer from the tariff frontiers,
twelve cabins and a white light on the masthead,
with its house flag and a freeboard of 6", boys
running with mates' receipts and bills of lading,
carries kilderkin imperial kegs and stingo firkins.

But the great turbo-electric ocean liner, fire-insured,
has circulating ice water swift for the belly,
and anchor hooks and forcign mail.

The Creator

Fresh mollusk morning
puts a foot out
from its bivalve
on the sea

and in a moment
the underwater
fairy palm blooms

and all the trout
and mussel
come to life

and wrasse and sturgeon
dart through the water
with their hungry heads.

What have I brought home
in the skin of the sea cucumber
that looks like wheels and anchors
under the microscope?

The Night Watch

An ambulance with modest glass doors
and a silver cross arrives
with naked clerks, importers, barbers,
gunsmiths, glassblowers, goldbeaters,
old men from hotels, pink and tailored,
naphtha-smelling Irish priests,
cravat-and-boy face of the movie usher,
Frankel, Shmulik, Old Country watchmakers.

The whole city lies here, illuminated
on the operating table
for the surgeon and his delicate
nickel-plated instruments.

And all the people are one sea water,
one circulatory system of man
observing his magnificent urea.

The Classes

1

One hour from here a loggia
above the pepper trees,
a tiny cascade, and vines
above the bath house,
men and women driving
on the fairway, laughing,
surrounded by Galloway
pottery, garden furniture
and white daisies.

Under this Luxemburg of heaven

orangerie and game room,
Old English tall twisted
stem-engraved goblets

Royal Copenhagen porcelain,
mutton-fat jade Chien Lung bowl

a toilet bottle
                    amethyst
stopper & a monogram shield.

2

Immigrants from Lodz
in a furnished room
close to the stores.

Porcelain pitcher,
bath and hand towels
on the bed rails.

A new sign goes into the window:
Smocking, Hemstitching, Rhinestone Setting.

Waiting for a Poem

How keen the night was!
Not a star out
nor a sparrow.

When at last
I felt as high
and keen as the night

I took a swan dive
but I must have got
my signals crossed

for I lost
what I was after
from star to sparrow.

Sea-kin, I have broken away.
My heart has risen like a bird
in the waterways and breaks into words.
May I have a true and easy course!

The Disillusionment
of a Very Young Man

There is nothing
to a woman
but a bitter earth

and in a poem
nothing but the small head
of a sparrow.

Tell me
is not every man
his own host
juggling rabbits,
eggs, bananas?

On the esplanade at Cannes
the awnings suddenly
went black before me.

I was carried to the belvedere
of Villa Policastro.
In the evening in the sight
of blood and bandages
I lay there like a dressed fowl.

An ideal sang like a canary
on a marble seat above the Ligurian
for the early grapes
and apple blossoms of heaven
where the heart I hope is lighter.

An Old Fiction

In the salt warp
was the plasma,
in the springhead
and the sulphurous water.

Jupiter the sire hawk
flew through Athens.
Then the Greeks sang
and the wings turned
through the light.

We sat upon a stone
with happy records,
shipping kelp and sulphur
through the islands.

Athens was a hawk.

Then there was Corinth,
once a pedestal for wrestlers
in classical shorts.
What method in their manner!

Shall we say the gods
with lights behind us
broke wind in a changing system?

Yesterday behind the olive boughs
they seemed so lucid!

NOTES

ABBREVIATIONS USED IN THE NOTES

CHC   Contempo Records, Southern Historical Collection, Library of the University of North Carolina at Chapel Hill

CP   *Poetry* Magazine Papers, 1912–1936, University of Chicago Library

MR   Rakosi Archive, Department of Special Collections, Memorial Library, University of Wisconsin-Madison

MT   Parker Tyler (ed.), *Modern Things*, The Galleon Press: NY 1934

NP   *Pagany* Papers, University of Delaware Library, Newark, Delaware

PW   August Derleth and Raymond E.F. Larsson (eds.), *Poetry out of Wisconsin*, Henry Harrisson: NY 1937

SP   Carl Rakosi, *Selected Poems*, New Directions: Norfolk, Conn. 1941

YL   Margery Latimer Papers, Yale Collection of American Literature, Beinecke Rare Book and Manuscript Library, Yale University

YP   Ezra Pound Papers, Yale Collection of American Literature, Beinecke Rare Book and Manuscript Library, Yale University

Editorial Introduction

1. Rakosi's name appeared in the lists of writers for future publication printed on the covers of books published by To, Publishers and The Objectivist Press; see, for example, William Carlos Williams, *A Novelette and Other Prose* (To, Publishers, 1932), and *Collected Poems 1921–1932* (The Objectivist Press, 1934).

2. Margery Latimer, letter to Carl Rakosi (August 1931): YL; Carl Rakosi, postcard to Ezra Pound (September 1932): YP.

3. Carl Rakosi, "Carl Rakosi", in *Contemporary Authors Autobiography Series* Vol. 5, Gale Research Co.: Detroit 1987.

4. Louis Aragon, "What a Divine Being" [translation of "Quelle âme divine", in Aragon, *Le Libertinage,* Paris 1924], *The Issue* 1,2 (Feb. 1926). (English translations of Aragon had earlier been published in *Broom, The Little Review*, and *Secession*.) *The Issue: A Forum of Student Opinion* was published at the University of Wisconsin: two numbers (December 1925 and February 1926) appeared under the editorship of Carl Rakosi and Louis Schindler; one number of a second volume, under different editorship, appeared in December 1926. The magazine discussed educational policy in the light of the collapse of Progressive politics following La Follette's unsuccessful campaign in the 1924 presidential election. Rakosi's contribution to this discussion (under the pseudonym "Oswald Tweed") was less than starry eyed about Wisconsin exceptionalism. "In some Wisconsin factory towns a man is ashamed to walk the streets with a book under his arm. Out of that environment grows the feeling that society is a mob, grinding the artist's passion and imagination under foot. And when he sails out of New York, on his way to the Old World, his relief will be expressed by something like, 'Gentlemen, hats off to the cult of the moron.'" ("The Cult of the Moron", *The*

Issue 1,2.) Rakosi would appear to have been thinking of going to Russia at this time (Latimer, letter to Carl Rakosi [April 1926]: YL.)

5. For Zukofsky's opinion of Crane see "American Poetry 1920–1930" in *Prepositions: The Collected Critical Essays of Louis Zukofsky*, University of California Press: Berkeley 1981.

6. Carl Rakosi, postcard to Morton Dauwen Zabel (June 1933): CP.

7. The League of American Writers, *Writers Take Sides: Letters about the war in Spain from 418 American authors*, NY 1938.

8. Kenneth Fearing, letter to Carl Rakosi [1940]: Harry Ransom Humanities Research Center, University of Texas at Austin.

9. Carl Rakosi, "Plans for Work": Archives of the John Simon Guggenheim Memorial Foundation.

Poems 1923–1941

Information of various sorts is included in the following notes. They follow the same chronological order of publication as the text, so that some poems are grouped together according to their initial publication. Details of subsequent publication, and of manuscripts, are also recorded: in some cases such detail relates to poems initially published together, but in others it relates to separate poems from such groups, and these are the subject of subordinate notes, indicated by indentation of the poem's title. The copy text is listed first in all cases, and thus sometimes appears before the particulars of initial publication. Differences between text and copy text (although of the sort normally corrected in silence) are noted, as are significant variants in other printed or manuscript sources. Other information, concerning dates of composition, for example, or Rakosi's connections with the magazines in which he published, is included in appropriate places.

Jacob Gold; The Old Men
The Wisconsin Literary Magazine XXII,6 (April 1923)

              JACOB GOLD
4   creatures] creatures.

Gigantic Walker
The Liberator 6,5 (May 1923)

Two Digging; Six Essays in Sentiment
The Wisconsin Literary Magazine XXIII,1 (October 1923)

Two Digging

14   kettle,] kettle
20   Janik] Janick
25   down on] down..on
34   Janik] Vanik
50   waited] waite
67   dollars,] dollars
78   sun.] sun
84   the doorway] the he doorway
85   rather] rathr
103   motion,] motion

Six Essays in Sentiment

1.4   above.)] above)
1.6   came] come
1.8   day.)] day)
3.2   and] an
3.4   bough] bow
6   *Choleric*] *Choloric*

Plein-Air
The Wisconsin Literary Magazine XXIII,2 (November 1923)

5   squirrels] Squirrels

Idyll of Seeds; The Flowers of Gloom
The Wisconsin Literary Magazine XXIII,3 (December 1923)

Idyll of Seeds

7   cicadas] cicidas
14   head.)] head)
End note] *Excerpt from Convalescence*

The Flowers of Gloom

3   Oh] O

For Lothario
The Daily Cardinal (March 30, 1924)

For the Processionals of Lust
Palms I,6 (1924)
    1   blond] blonde
    6   sleep.)] sleep).

Creation
Palms II,4 (1924)
    2   apple...sky] Apple...Sky
    3   berries] Berries
    7   the] The

Sittingroom by Patinka; The January of a Gnat; Flora and the Ogre
The Little Review XI,1 (Spring 1925)

                    SITTINGROOM BY PATINKA
    18   passions.] passions."
    36   prophecy] prophesy

                    FLORA AND THE OGRE
    12   (Linen] (linen
    13   like...veins.)] Like...veins)

The Holy Bonds
The Nation CXXI,3155 (December 23, 1925)

Autumn in Dane County
The Issue 1,1 (December 1925)
    7   fire.] fire
The New Student 9,13 (January 6, 1926)

Hokku
The Echo 4,2 (March 1926)

Shadows for Florida
The Nation CXXII,3174 (May 5, 1926)

Scriptural Program
Two Worlds 1,4 (June 1926)

1.9	books] books;
1.11	Palestine);] Palestine)
6.3	shoulders.] shoulders
7.26	eyes.] eyes

Vitagraph
The New Masses 4 (August 1926)

Margery Latimer suggested that Rakosi send poems to James Rorty, editor of *The New Masses*, and subsequently drew his attention to three other new publications: *The Exile, The American Caravan*, and *transition*. (Letters to Carl Rakosi [March 1926 and September 1927]: YL.)

Characters; Wanted; Superproduction; Revue
The Exile 2, (Autumn 1927)

Impressions
The American Caravan, A Yearbook of American Literature, The Macauley Company: NY 1927

Dolce Padre and Ephebus; The Founding of New Hampshire
TMSS: YP
transition 12 (March 1928)

DOLCE PADRE AND EPHEBUS
Pagany II,2 (April–June 1931)

Extracts from a Private Life
The Exile 4 (Autumn 1928)

| 2.5 | koranmen)] koranmen.) |
| 2.7 | gallery).] gallery.) |

Orphean Lost; Fluteplayers from Finmarken; Unswerving Marine;
Before You
Poetry XXXVII,V (February 1931)

	FLUTEPLAYERS FROM FINMARKEN
6	swandive.)] swandive).
20	rock.)] rock).

TMS: YP

2	Svensen.] Svensen,
3	Not] not
8	seal bones] perchlungs,
10	rock-cistvaen] rockcistvaen
11	grief-stricken] griefstricken
17	(There...pigeon] (Because...a
18	or...sight.] pigeon or...sight,
19	My] my
30	arrived:] arrived.....
31	musing] musing from
32	from one] one

Revue; Death Song; [Dolce Padre and Ephebus]
Pagany II,2 (April–June 1931)

Louis Zukofsky offered to send on to *Pagany* and *Hound and
Horn* any poems he did not want for the "Objectivists" number of
Poetry. (Letter to Carl Rakosi [November 17, 1930] in Rakosi's notes
on his correspondence with Zukofsky: MR.) Rakosi wrote to Rich-
ard Johns, editor of *Pagany*, "Glad to come out in Pagany. Do you
mind making the following changes? In "Out of the Egg" cut out
the whole windy title, please, and merely call the poem "SALONS".
I am sending you new versions of "News" (now called WE), Sylvia
(with the rest of the title out), and Revue. I hope, for god sake, you
use them in place of the old. In fact, don't show the old ones to
anyone!" (Undated, late 1930 or early 1931: NP.)

REVUE
10   me."] me.

DEATH SONG
5   Behold] behold

Sylvia; Salons; The Athletes
Pagany II,4 (October–December 1931)

SALONS

TMS: YP

Title] Out of the Egg or The Works of Farter Flute
4   rib bones] ribbones
9   shadows, and] shadows and
16   fats] brasses
17   fellowship, which] fellowship which

THE ATHLETES
31   shellacked] shellaced

Amulet; Song; Sealight; Handel; Paraguay
Poetry XXXIX,II (November 1931)

Rakosi wrote to Harriet Monroe, the editor of *Poetry*, "Not wishing to give the group a pretentious or decorative title, I shall be satisfied with 'Early Poems' or 'Early Work'. [...] I believe the proper order for the poems is (1) Amulet, (2) Song, (3) Sealight, (4) Handel, and (5) Paraguay." (Undated, before June 1931: CP.) The poems were published under the title "The Littoral", in the sequence (following Rakosi's numbering) 5,1,3,2,4.

Frankfort and Bethlehem; Paris; Foyer, The Orpheum
Pagany III,1 (January–March 1932)

FOYER, THE ORPHEUM
13   God).] God)

A Journey Away; Parades
   Louis Zukofsky (ed.), *An "Objectivists" Anthology*, To, Publishers: Le Beausset (Var) and New York 1932

A JOURNEY AWAY
    4.10   armor,] armor
    5.6   stone,] stone?
    5.19   Bargello] Bardello
    9.9   Sir."] Sir.".
Hound and Horn v,4 (July–September 1932)
         [Sections 7,4,5,6,8,1,9, numbered 1–7]

PW

         [Section 5]
         Title] From "Intimate Studies": 3

PARADES
    7   in] In
TMS: CHC
         Title] Parades [*deleted* : African Theme, Needlework, Etc.]

African Theme, Needlework, Etc.
Contact 1,3 (October 1932)
    Lines 2.9–10 are transposed in the copy text, apparently in error when the galleys were made up into pages. In *PW* lines 11–12 precede lines 9–10, an ingenious attempt to make sense from nonsense. *SP* adopts the simpler solution preferred here.

         [Section 2]

PW

         Title] Needlework
         13–15 *omitted*

The Islands
The Lion and Crown 1,1 (Fall 1932)

      27   ink.] ink
      33   (Oilburn] (oilburn

Lines 1–2 occurred in a poem Rakosi sent to Margery Latimer early in 1931, and were quoted in her reply. (Letter to Carl Rakosi [March 1931]: YL.)

Happy New Year
The Windsor Quarterly 1,1 (Spring 1933)

The Memoirs
TMS: CP
Poetry XLII,1 (April 1933)
PW

Good Prose
The New Act 2 (June 1933)
TMS: YP
TMS: YL

      15   his biscuit and his seed] his seed and his biscuit
      17   wetting waxy] tapering ferocious
      Extra line] Arise, beloved.

Rakosi sent this poem to Margery Latimer by August 1932.

Sappho; The Classics; The Gnat; The Wedding
The Windsor Quarterly 1,2 (Summer 1933)

"The Gnat" is a reworking of "The January of a Gnat"; Zukofsky's "mirror fugue" upon it (dated Thanksgiving, 1932) was published in the same number of *The Windsor Quarterly*.

THE CLASSICS

PW

THE WEDDING

MT

Men on Yachts; The Lobster
Carl Rakosi, *Two Poems*, Modern Editions Press: New York [1933]
The Westminster Magazine 22 (Autumn 1933)
PW

Williams's "Rhymed address to Carl Rakosi acknowledging (with thanks) the excellence of his poem *The Lobster*" (*Collected Poems* I, 364–5) was published in the same number of *The Westminster Magazine*.

MEN ON YACHTS

The Westminster Magazine

       Title] The Men Fled Military Service
    24   The men fled military service in the Empire.]
    The   Empire.

PW

    Title] Ennui
    7 *omitted*
    12   onion stew and cart hack,] men fled military service.
    16   limited] Limited
    24 *omitted*

Line 16 is set to the margin, and line 17 ranged beneath line 12 to align and contrast "Along the Danube" and "Along the Boston Limited", "military service" and "commercial service".

THE LOBSTER

    6   rising.] rising
    7   Plasma—] plasma
    26   vertebrae] vertebra

The Westminster Magazine

    26   [vertebrae]
    31   Saltflush] Saltfish

SP

    31   Salflush lobster] Salt-flush lobster bull,
    32   bull encrusted] encrusted,

The Beasts
MT
Poetry XLIII,III (November 1933)
3.12   glassware, like] glassware for
TMS: CP
PW
[Sections 1 and 3 only, unnumbered]

This is presumably the poem mentioned by Rakosi in a letter to Ezra Pound, "I'm at work (in the minutest spasms) on a longish thing, of which, also, I can send you the first four or five pages". (Undated, before June 1931: YP.) Rakosi sent "The Beasts" to Richard Johns for *Pagany* by the Summer of 1932, but *Pagany* ceased publication; he then made cuts for its publication in *Poetry* (letter to Morton Dauwen Zabel [December 19, 1932]: CP). Before its appearance in *Poetry* portions cut from the original had been published as "Men on Yachts" and "The Wedding".

The choice of copy text for this important poem requires explanation. The *Poetry* version was corrupted by over-zealous copy editing, and in the MS it is impossible to distinguish with complete certainty which autograph markings are editorial and which (if any) are authorial. The version in *Modern Things* follows the MS in all significant respects, and was probably taken from a carbon copy. *Poetry* prints a dash at the end of line 1.3, and this was retained in *Modern Things*, but is here emended to hyphenate "sea-cucumber". Hyphenation throughout may be editorial in origin, but although in *Selected Poems* "sea cucumber" is not hyphenated ("The Creator") the form "cravat-and-boy face" (which might more conventionally be written "cravat and boy-face") is retained ("The Night Watch").

The Poem; National Winter Garden Shamrock
The New Act 3 (April 1934)

The Black Crow
Negro, An Anthology, Collected and edited by Nancy Cunard, Wishart: London 1934

Country People Never Learn; To My First Born; Pike Eater's Song;
The People; To the Non-Political Citizen; To a Collie Pup; Decla-
ration; To an Anti-Semite; Dedication
SP

> TO MY FIRST BORN
7   love?'"] love'?"

> THE PEOPLE
14   me and] my and

Appendix: Unpublished, Never Completed, and Revised Poems

Travels Among the Yakahulas
TMS: YP

    Another MS at Yale provides a revised version of Stanza 3, later
incorporated in the version of this poem published as "Sylvia".

A Predilection
TMS: YP

    Unsigned, but with the other Rakosi papers in the Ezra Pound
papers at Yale, and apparently typed on the same machine as the
Yale MS of "Good Prose".

Equations
TMS: CHC

The Beasts [Reconstruction]

    This reconstruction of the original version of "The Beasts" is in-
complete, but provides a guide to the conception and scope of the
poem before cuts were made for its publication in *Poetry*. Rakosi's
letter to Zabel (see note on "The Beasts", above) enables some can-
celled passages to be identified and inserted, but the opening lines
remain unidentified, and the passage from "This private enterprise"
(a line supplied from Rakosi's letter to Zabel) and "stopper & a

monogram shield" is almost certainly incomplete. For the purpose of this reconstruction I have used the typewritten MS of "The Beasts" (CP) as copy text, but ignored punctuation added thereto by hand. It has not been possible to locate a MS of the original version. For a full account of the evidence on which the reconstruction is based see the editor's "Remembering Carl Rakosi: A Conjectural Reconstruction of 'The Beasts'", in Michael Heller (ed.), *Carl Rakosi, Man and Poet*, The National Poetry Foundation: Orono, Maine 1993.

The Old Men; Heroes Bought and Sold; A Dollar is a Man's Best Friend; The Legion; To Pa Coughlin
AMSS and TMSS: MR

These unfinished drafts from circa 1938 fall into two groups. One deals with the position of the intelligentsia in the class structure of market capitalism, the other with the poet's response to the rise and appeasement of fascism and the collapse of civilised values. The titles are Rakosi's but the texts represent an editorial attempt to establish the main contours along which Rakosi's drafts tended to stabilise.

The first three poems show different aspects of several folios of undifferentiated manuscript. As Rakosi's phrases proliferate and interbreed (so that avatars of the "old men" include "purse bearers" and "button pushers") thematic emphasis shifts between the wealth and power of the ruling class, the corruption of values, and the honesty of the people. The interlocutory rhetoric of these drafts is indicative of the position Rakosi adopted as a writer on the left, but its boundaries shift as he works his way through the standard terms of communist class analysis. This rhetorical instability, which may explain why these drafts were never brought to a satisfactory conclusion, is vividly revealed in one of them where, following a series of lines in the first person plural of "Heroes Bought and Sold", the writing breaks into the first person singular.

> Enough, enough. I change the person to you malcontents.
>   Oh honest malcontents
> I find my male self in your common touch
> yr. great intimate encounters
> Let us find our male self again
> Let us be curious about these ind. patriots who designate—

The first four sections of "The Legion" exist in draft typescript. The remainder comes from an associated autograph manuscript so closely worked that its patchwork appearance underscores the phrasal dependence of Rakosi's rhetoric in these unfinished political poems. The last three lines are placed thus in order to lend the series of parallel clauses some grammatical closure. The title is taken from the same manuscript, where the two words appear in somewhat prominent isolation. "To Pa Coughlin" is a separate typewritten draft, the title added in autograph.

Associated with these drafts is an autograph manuscript bearing the date 9.20.38 and headed "On the proposed partition of Czechoslovakia" and "Black day". This manuscript begins with a reference to Chamberlain, associated no doubt with the well known newsreel images of his return from Munich, and continues as a series of prose memoranda for a poem in which the phrase "black day" was to be repeated.

> This gangling ninny wears a laurel, the honor of having
>   [wiped out Cze—
> Yesterday you and I were of no importance
> Today whole nations are of no importance, wiped out by
>   [negotiation
> Yesterday a man here or there knew injustice—
> now whole nations know no justice

> Theme: this can not be 1938, this is not my city, not my land

Around me whirls the Ind. Rev., the French Rev., the
Renaissance, etc.—All as if had never been—
I am back in the Ghetto
with a yellow Jewsign on my back
the streets have >
the women watch the pots and conceive children—
there is no thought that one worker is related to another
that he's a worker—he just happens to be who he is
working at what he's working

the very air is choking—I am like a drowned man bloated with
water (bloated with feeling)—it has entered my mouth and
puffed me out into a balloon of frustration—choked up
      [like a
drowned man (to thrice my size)
A limit to degradation

Every honest word = Red
& every intense passion Jewish
curious tenacity = not so curious after all—has >
something precious
strangely precious
the curious intensity of Communists—homely & sweet
their many tongues
gives me a feeling of security
people's salute
raised fist
the public speaking
the meeting tonight

There is no beauty in the world—I find no rest & toss
      [tormented
I am deprived of manhood—how find it?
No, I will not go back to the [*deleted* Ghetto] Middle Ages.

Surrealists (1930); The Wedding; The Status Quo; Poetry; Ships;
The Creator; The Night Watch; The Classes; Waiting for a Poem;
The Disillusionment of a Very Young Man; An Old Fiction
SP

These versions exceed normal revision: they are new poems pro-
duced by amalgamation and condensation of old ones. For "Surre-
alists (1930)" compare "Foyer, The Orpheum" and "The Athletes";
for "The Status Quo": "The Beasts"; for "Poetry": "The Beasts" 3;
for "Ships": "A Journey Away" 9 and "Happy New Year"; for "The
Creator": "The Beasts" 1; for "The Night Watch" and "The Classes":
"The Beasts" and "The Wedding"; for "Waiting for a Poem": "A
Journey Away" 7 and "Fluteplayers from Finmarken"; for "The Dis-
illusionment of a Very Young Man": "A Journey Away" 3, "Before
You", and "Extracts from a Private Life" 5; for "An Old Fiction":
"The Islands" and "Before You".

Selected Poems

Rakosi wrote to James Laughlin on October 17, 1940, to inquire
into the possibility of publishing with New Directions. Laughlin
offered him a place in the new "Poet of the Month" series, and
Selected Poems went through the press in December 1941.

Rakosi's letters to Laughlin are factually misleading and self-con-
tradictory; like *Selected Poems* they display a degree of uncertainty
about what he had done as a poet. In his first letter Rakosi refers to
poems written between 1921 and 1931, which he has "gone
over...giving them a good barbering." He also says that he stopped
writing in 1931, and that only three of the poems are unpublished.
In a second letter, dated November 12, 1940, Rakosi speaks of with-
holding thirteen unpublished poems for magazine publication. A
third letter, dated November 12, 1940, offers a free choice of poems,
apparently at Laughlin's suggestion. In fact *Selected Poems* includes
little that was published before 1931, and includes poems written in

the late 1930s, two of which ("To My First Born" and "To a Collie Pup") were presumably written after Rakosi's first approach to Laughlin. It is likely that Rakosi was not writing in the mid-1930s, and his first letter to Laughlin is probably only a year or two out in its statement that he wrote nothing after 1931 if we understand this to discount the political poems of the late 1930s, although these are included in a list of unpublished poems in his second letter.

The following poems, in addition to those included from it in this edition, appeared in *Selected Poems*: "The Classics", "The Young Man" ("A Journey Away" 2), "Vitagraph", "Amulet", "Early American Chronicle" ("The Memoirs"), "The Lobster", "The Concert" ("A Journey Away" 5), "Family Likeness" ("A Journey Away" 4), "A Bit of Hardy" ("A Journey Away" 1), "Needlework", "News from the old Country" ("Extracts from a Private Life" 1), "The Winter Garden" ("National Winter Garden Shamrock"), "Lamp" ("The Beasts" 1.42–50); "Woman" ("Sappho"); "Good Prose"; "A Surrealist Conception of Paris" ("Paris" 2–4), "Institutions" ("The Beasts" 1.33–41). Variants arising from "barbering" have not been noted.

INDEX OF TITLES AND FIRST LINES

A Bohemian idea   96
A cutter risen from the mollusks, it is a god   112
A little river steamer from the tariff frontiers,   111
A slender plank above a waterhole,   74
A technical display.   88
A yellow feather   113
AFRICAN THEME, NEEDLEWORK, ETC.   107
After the bath she touched her hair   122
After the jostling on canal streets   92
AMULET   90
An ambulance with modest glass doors   174
THE ATHLETES   88
AUTUMN IN DANE COUNTRY   55

THE BEASTS   126
THE BEASTS [Reconstruction]   151
BEFORE YOU   82
Before you is Corinth—   82
Between the two gold   168
THE BLACK CROW   135
But you are ideal,   90

CHARACTERS   66
THE CLASSES   175
THE CLASSICS   117
Clear me with this master music when   87
COUNTRY PEOPLE NEVER LEARN   136
CREATION   49
THE CREATOR   173

Daladier, Hitler, Chamberlain, Mussolini 164
DEATH SONG 85
DECLARATION 142
DEDICATION 144
THE DISSILLUSIONMENT OF A VERY YOUNG MAN 178
Do not come among these trees of lead. 49
DOLCE PADRE AND EPHEBUS 72
A DOLLAR IS A MAN'S BEST FRIEND 161
During the water movement 97
During the water movement of the French horns 166

Easter sea, 100 fathoms, 124
EQUATIONS 149
Every man is entitled to his anger. 140
Expert experiences black on white 67
EXTRACTS FROM A PRIVATE LIFE 75

FLORA AND THE OGRE 53
THE FLOWERS OF GLOOM 46
FLUTEPLAYERS FROM FINMARKEN 79
FOR LOTHARIO 47
FOR THE PROCESSIONALS OF LUST 48
THE FOUNDING OF NEW HAMPSHIRE 74
FOYER, THE ORPHEUM 97
FRANKFORT AND BETHLEHEM 95
Fresh mollusk morning 173
Fresh mollusk morning puts a foot 126, 151
From Sinai to Killarney, a comic burst, 84

GIGANTIC WALKER 35
THE GNAT 119
God, if I were up so high, 35
GOOD PROSE 113
Gray light bereaved the calm all day; 46

HANDEL 93
HAPPY NEW YEAR 111
Heavenly father, 72
HEROES BOUGHT AND SOLD 159
HOKKU 56
THE HOLY BONDS 54
How keen the night was! 177
How keen the nights were, 79

I felt your foot below your mother's breast 137
I found Miss Levi in a plush repose, 50
I saw the knotted old men gaze 34
I shall put my purity away now 142
I walked out ten miles on our mall of willows 55
IDYLL OF SEEDS 44
If the button-pushers with their high-toned secretaries 161
IMPRESSIONS 70
In the early hours the lovebirds 94
In the salt warp [AN OLD FICTION] 180
In the salt warp [THE ISLANDS] 109
THE ISLANDS 109
It is good to be here. 169
It is orchids 132

JACOB GOLD 33
Janik, a middle-aged Slovak... 36
THE JANUARY OF A GNAT 52
A JOURNEY AWAY 100

THE LEGION 162
Let her quince knees sag 53
Let us voice our opinions in the peace 159
THE LOBSTER 124
Lost in the still hair of the pine, 44
Lothario, I've ordered a winding sheet 47

THE MEMOIRS 112
MEN ON YACHTS 122
My bride presents me with a chart of gall 54
My Venice: modern Europe and Siam 148

NATIONAL WINTER GARDEN SHAMROCK 134
THE NIGHT WATCH 174

O you in whom distrust lies under 139
AN OLD FICTION 180
THE OLD MEN [l saw the knotted old men gaze] 34
THE OLD MEN [You must be wondering how they got there,] 158
Old men and expunged 56
One hour from here a loggia 175
One must have sullen wits 107
One must have sullen wits to foot the jungle 135
One o'clock. A rainy night. 172
One of our brassy beefeaters 66
ORPHEAN LOST 78
Out in God's country where men are men, 65

PARADES 106
PARAGUAY 94
PARIS 96
THE PEOPLE 139
PIKE-EATER'S SONG 138
PLEIN-AIR 43
THE POEM 132
POETRY 171
A PREDILECTION 148

Return, sweet ladies, in aplomb and apostolic passage 106
REVUE [From Sinai to Killarney, a comic burst,] 84
REVUE [They say in dreams they have a peetweet's view] 69

St. Louis songbirds in Atlanta. 68
SALONS 87
SAPPHO 115
SCRIPTURAL PROGRAM 59
SEALIGHT 92
SHADOWS FOR FLORIDA 57
SHIPS 172
SITTINGROOM BY PATINKA 50
SIX ESSAYS IN SENTIMENT 40
Snow panels, ice pipes, house the afternoon 52
So you fought for the Jews 143
SONG 91
Spin a dream of the woman you love. 40
THE STATUS QUO 169
steps out 115
Summer, the Negro's cabin was full of voices, 57
SUPERPRODUCTION 68
SURREALISTS (1930) 166
SYLVIA 86

The blazing crocus 134
The bridge-hands at the edge of the water, 43
The eyes are centered here 70
The girls 117
The hours 138
The king of the Jews shall understand 59
The oakboughs of the cottagers 78
The piccolo of heaven 93
The tree and the stone are the only Nordics 149
The way you look up at me 141
The wayfarer met the passerby 100
There is nothing 178
They are the same everywhere. 136
They say in dreams they have a peetweet's view 69

This blond youth like an acolyte makes hue   48
This is in the wind;   81
This postcard has the Christmas   95
TO A COLLIE PUP   141
TO AN ANTI-SEMITE   143
TO MY FIRST BORN   137
TO PA COUGHLIN   164
to the house   144
TO THE NON-POLITICAL CITIZEN   140
TRAVELS AMONG THE YAKAHULAS   147
Trot out the circus barkers, ladies, clowns,   147
Trot out the negro singers, ladies, clowns   86
Turning as from an instrument   91
TWO DIGGING   36

Under this Luxemburg of heaven   120
UNSWERVING MARINE   81

VITAGRAPH   65

WAITING FOR A POEM   177
WANTED   67
THE WEDDING [Between the two gold]   168
THE WEDDING [Under this Luxemburg of heaven]   120
What phantom men would wink behind his face?   33
When Hirohito writes on New Year's, "Peaceful   162
When the light sprang from the sea, blowing,   171
Winter and wind,   119

You must be wondering how they got there,   158
Young utopia of spring-greens,   85
Your second cousin, an obscure cigar maker from Smyrna,   75

CARL RAKOSI

Born in Berlin in 1903, educated in Hungary, and brought to the United States at the age of six, Carl Rakosi began writing poetry in his early twenties, and was well known in the 1930s as a member of the Objectivist Group, which also included William Carlos Williams, Louis Zukofsky, Charles Reznikoff, and George Oppen. New Directions published his *Selected Poems* in 1941.

When the Depression occurred, however, Rakosi gradually stopped writing, and fell into literary silence, disillusioned with the state of our society, where he felt there was no place for a poet.

In 1965 Rakosi once again began to write poetry, with New Directions publishing a collection, *Amulet*, in 1967 and his *Ere-Voice* in 1968. In 1975 Black Sparrow Press published Rakosi's *Ex Cranium Night* and in 1976 published *My Experiences in Parnassus. Droles de Journal* appeared from The Toothpaste Press in 1981. The National Poetry Foundation collected Rakosi's prose in 1983 and collected previously published and revised versions of his poems in *The Collected Poems* in 1986. The current edition collects Rakosi's poems, previously published and unpublished, from 1923–1941 as they originally appeared in print and/or, when available, in manuscript. Rakosi lives today in San Francisco.

SUN & MOON CLASSICS

This publication was made possible, in part, through an operational grant from the Andrew W. Mellon Foundation and through contributions from the following individuals and organizations:

Tom Ahern (Foster, Rhode Island)
Charles Altieri (Seattle, Washington)
John Arden (Galway, Ireland)
Paul Auster (Brooklyn, New York)
Jesse Huntley Ausubel (New York, New York)
Luigi Ballerini (Los Angeles, California)
Dennis Barone (West Hartford, Connecticut)
Jonathan Baumbach (Brooklyn, New York)
Roberto Bedoya (Los Angeles, California)
Guy Bennett (Los Angeles, California)
Bill Berkson (Bolinas, California)
Steve Benson (Berkeley, California)
Charles Bernstein and Susan Bee (New York, New York)
Dorothy Bilik (Silver Spring, Maryland)
Alain Bosquet (Paris, France)
In Memoriam: John Cage
In Memoriam: Camilo José Cela
Bill Corbett (Boston, Massachusetts)
Robert Crosson (Los Angeles, California)
Tina Darragh and P. Inman (Greenbelt, Maryland)
Fielding Dawson (New York, New York)
Christopher Dewdney (Toronto, Canada)
Larry Deyah (New York, New York)
Arkadii Dragomoschenko (St. Petersburg, Russia)
George Economou (Norman, Oklahoma)
Richard Elman (Stony Brook, New York)
Kenward Elmslie (Calais, Vermont)
Elaine Equi and Jerome Sala (New York, New York)
Lawrence Ferlinghetti (San Francisco, California)
Richard Foreman (New York, New York)
Howard N. Fox (Los Angeles, California)
Jerry Fox (Aventura, Florida)
In Memoriam: Rose Fox
Melvyn Freilicher (San Diego, California)
Miro Gavran (Zagreb, Croatia)
Allen Ginsberg (New York, New York)

Peter Glassgold (Brooklyn, New York)
Barbara Guest (Berkeley, California)
Perla and Amiram V. Karney (Bel Air, California)
Václav Havel (Prague, The Czech Republic)
Lyn Hejinian (Berkeley, California)
Fanny Howe (La Jolla, California)
Harold Jaffe (San Diego, California)
Ira S. Jaffe (Albuquerque, New Mexico)
Ruth Prawer Jhabvala (New York, New York)
Pierre Joris (Albany, New York)
Alex Katz (New York, New York)
Tom LaFarge (New York, New York)
Mary Jane Lafferty (Los Angeles, California)
Michael Lally (Santa Monica, California)
Norman Lavers (Jonesboro, Arkansas)
Jerome Lawrence (Malibu, California)
Stacey Levine (Seattle, Washington)
Herbert Lust (Greenwich, Connecticut)
Norman MacAffee (New York, New York)
Rosemary Macchiavelli (Washington, DC)
In Memoriam: Mary McCarthy
Harry Mulisch (Amsterdam, The Netherlands)
Iris Murdoch (Oxford, England)
Martin Nakell (Los Angeles, California)
In Memoriam: bpNichol
NORLA (Norwegian Literature Abroad) (Oslo, Norway)
Claes Oldenburg (New York, New York)
Toby Olson (Philadelphia, Pennsylvania)
Maggie O'Sullivan (Hebden Bridge, England)
Rochelle Owens (Norman, Oklahoma)
Bart Parker (Providence, Rhode Island)
Marjorie and Joseph Perloff (Pacific Palisades, California)
Dennis Phillips (Los Angeles, California)
Carl Rakosi (San Francisco, California)
Tom Raworth (Cambridge, England)
David Reed (New York, New York)
Ishmael Reed (Oakland, California)
Tom Roberdeau (Los Angeles, California)
Janet Rodney (Santa Fe, New Mexico)
Joe Ross (Washington, DC)
Jerome and Diane Rothenberg (Encinitas, California)
Edward Ruscha (Los Angeles, California)

If you would like to be a contributor to this series, please send your tax-deduct-ible contribution to The Contemporary Arts Educational Project, Inc., a non-profit corporation, 6026 Wilshire Boulevard, Los Angeles, California 90036.

SUN & MOON CLASSICS

AUTHOR   TITLE

Alferi, Pierre   *Natural Gait* 95 ($10.95)
Antin, David   *Selected Poems: 1963–1973* 10 ($12.95)
Barnes, Djuna   *At the Roots of the Stars: The Short Plays* 53
                                ($12.95)
                                The Book of Repulsive Women 59 ($6.95)
                                Collected Stories 110 ($24.95) (cloth)
                                Interviews 86 ($13.95)
                                New York 5 ($12.95)
                                Smoke and Other Early Stories 2 ($10.95)
Bernstein, Charles   *Content's Dream: Essays 1975–1984* 49
                                ($14.95)
                                Dark City 48 ($11.95)
                                Rough Trades 14 ($10.95)
Bjørneboe, Jens   *The Bird Lovers* 43 ($9.95)
du Bouchet, André   *Where Heat Looms* 87 ($11.95)
Breton, André   *Arcanum 17* 51 ($12.95)
                                Earthlight 26 ($12.95)
Bromige, David   *The Harbormaster of Hong Kong* 32
                                ($10.95)
Butts, Mary   *Scenes from the Life of Cleopatra* 72
                                ($13.95)
Cadiot, Olivier   *L'Art Poétique* 98 ($10.95)
Celan, Paul   *Breathturn* 74 ($12.95)
Coolidge, Clark   *The Crystal Text* 99 ($11.95)
                                Own Face 39 ($10.95)
                                The Rova Improvisations 34 ($11.95)
Copioli, Rosita   *The Blazing Lights of the Sun* 84 ($11.95)
De Angelis, Milo   *Finite Intuition* 65 ($11.95)
DiPalma, Ray   *Numbers and Tempers: Selected Early Poems*
                                24 (11.95)

von Doderer, Heimito	*The Demons* 13 ($29.95)
	Every Man a Murderer 66 ($14.95)
Donoso, José	*Hell Without Limits* 101 ($12.95)
Dragomoschenko, Arkadii	*Description* 9 ($11.95)
	Xenia 29 ($12.95)
Eça de Queiroz, José Maria de	*The City and the Mountains* 108 ($12.95)
Federman, Raymond	*Smiles on Washington Square* 60 ($10.95)
Firbank, Ronald	*Santal* 58 ($7.95)
Fourcade, Dominique	*Click-Rose* 94 ($10.95)
	Xbo 35 ($9.95)
Freud, Sigmund	*Delusion and Dream in* Gradiva 38 ($13.95)
Gilliams, Maurice	*Elias, or The Struggle with the Nightingales* 79 ($12.95)
Giraudon, Liliane	*Pallaksch, Pallaksch* 61 ($12.95)
Giuliani, Alfredo, ed	*I Novissimi* 55 ($14.95)
Greenwald, Ted	*The Licorice Chronicles* 97 ($12.95)
Guest, Barbara	*Defensive Rapture* 30 ($11.95)
Hamsun, Knut	*Victoria* 69 ($10.95)
	Wayfarers 88 ($13.95)
Hardy, Thomas	*Jude the Obscure* 77 ($12.95)
Haugen, Paal-Helge	*Wintering with the Light* 107 ($11.95)
Hauser, Marianne	*Me & My Mom* 36 ($9.95)
	Prince Ishmael 4 ($11.95)
Hawkes, John	*The Owl* and *The Goose on the Grave* 67 ($12.95)
Hejinian, Lyn	*The Cell* 21 ($11.95)
	The Cold of Poetry 42 ($12.95)
	My Life 11 ($9.95)
Hoel, Sigurd	*The Road to the World's End* 75 ($13.95)
Howe, Fanny	*Bronte Wilde (Radical Love: 1)* 82 ($12.95)
	The Deep North 15 ($9.95)
	Saving History 27 ($12.95)
Howe, Susan	*The Europe of Trusts* 7 ($10.95)